GOOD PRACTICE IN THE ACCREDITATION OF PRIOR LEARNING

Also available from Cassell:

P. Ainley and B. Bailey: *The Business of Learning*
N. Evans: *Experiential Learning for All*
L. Glover: *GNVQ into Practice*

Good Practice in the Accreditation of Prior Learning

Lovemore Nyatanga, Dawn Forman & Jane Fox

CASSELL

Cassell
Wellington House
125 Strand
London WC2R 0BB

PO Box 605
Herndon
VA 20172

First published 1998

British Library Cataloguing-in-Publication Data
A catalogue record for this book is available from the British Library.

ISBN 0-304-34650-0 (hardback)
      0-304-34651-9 (paperback)
Edited and typeset by Ruth Noble, Peebles, Scotland
Printed and bound in Great Britain by Redwood Books, Trowbridge, Wiltshire

Contents

Figures and Tables

Acknowledgements

The authors would like to acknowledge the help and support of a number of people who have made the production of this book possible.

First, we acknowledge the contribution made by Terry Rich not only to Part Two of this book but also for being a critical friend. Terry was instrumental in the provision of many of the candidate examples which have made the applied nature of this book more visible. Second, we acknowledge the contribution of Patricia Davis and the Nottingham City Council Development Department for permission to adapt the material in Part Two. We also wish to acknowledge the information technology expertise and contribution made by Allan Hopcraft. For instance, when we could not compress the document into one floppy disk for the publishers Allan came to the rescue. A few more people whose help made this book possible include Janice Dyer and Yvonne Gregson for typing some of the manuscripts, Dave Hiscock for arranging all the inter-library loans, particularly in the early stages of this work, Louise Kelsey for use of the portfolio assessments.

Last but not least we acknowledge the support and help of our publisher whose encouragement inspired the completion of this book, the Council for Adult and Experiential Learning (CAEL), the National Council for Education Technology (NCET), the British Lending Library (Boston Spa), Open University, and many colleges and universities for giving us the experience reflected in this book.

Introduction

The book will be of interest to those who wish to:

- Explore the theoretical basis to the Accreditation of Prior Learning (APL)
- Gain some practical insight into the various applications of APL
- Develop and apply principles of good practice in APL
- Consider the key elements underpinning quality assurance issues in APL.

In considering the wide range of awards from National Vocational Qualifications (NVQs) to Masters programmes, the authors have given equal consideration to the theoretical and practical aspects of APL. The intention throughout the book is to highlight elements of good practice. This has been achieved through the exploration of APL practice based mainly on the United Kingdom (UK). This is largely due to the authors' experience and the need to provide, in Part Two of this book, some worked examples of good practice. In order to maintain possible coherence of examples in Part Two, it was felt that the culture and underpinning policies had to be comparable. Some consideration, however, is given to the development of APL in other countries in particular the USA.

Good practice in the accreditation of prior learning implies sound understanding of the theoretical issues as well as good application to practice. To this end the book is presented in two parts. Part One will discuss mainly developmental and theoretical issues in APL while Part Two will focus mainly on application issues. The inclusion of Part Two is intended to demonstrate the comprehensiveness and complexity of the APL operations as well as show how the various elements of good practice can be realised.

The chapters themselves are presented as follows:
Chapters 1 to 6 offer the theoretical underpinnings of APL (see next paragraph). These six chapters will be particularly relevant to readers wishing to focus upon the debates and theories within APL.

Chapter 1 will consider the educational context of APL. This chapter will also give a brief comparative international perspective. Chapter 2 will consider the nature and variety of evidence. Chapter 3 will present the principles of assessment and the accreditation process, while quality assurance issues will be discussed in Chapter 4. Organisational factors in APL will be the central theme to Chapter 5, while APL as an evolving agenda is debated in Chapter 6. Being the final chapter of the theoretical perspectives, Chapter 6 will highlight some of the research within this area. It should enable the reader to see the range of issues being debated and how good practice may be facilitated or indeed hindered.

In contrast, Part Two assists those readers wishing to gain insights into the practical and operational aspects of APL. Part Two also starts with its own introduction to enable readers to turn directly to it. These chapters (7 and 8) contain worked examples of APL portfolio submissions made against a variety of academic awards. Chapter 7 is intended to highlight the application of APL to competency-based award and, in particular, the nature of portfolio evidence required to satisfy given learning outcomes. Chapter 8 is intended to highlight the overall quality assurance processes underpinning APL.

Part One

Conceptual Issues in the Accreditation of Prior Learning

Chapter 1

Educational Context of Good Practice

INTRODUCTION

Accreditation of Prior Learning (APL) emerged in the USA in the 1970s as a successful research project, 'Co-operative Assessment of Experiential Learning Project' at Educational Testing Service in Princeton, New Jersey. APL is now common place in America with colleges throughout all states offering APL as a real option. In the USA the Council for Adult and Experiential Learning (CAEL) has done a lot to promote principles of good APL practice. There is also evidence (Nyatanga 1993; Fugate and Chapman 1992) to suggest that in America, APL is gaining favour. Fugate and Chapman (1992) carried out a survey of 3,694 American institutions on behalf of CAEL. Their report suggests an upward trend in terms of interest and commitment to APL. Before turning to APL developments in the UK it may be useful just to state some of the early CAEL objectives that have helped in the establishment of an APL culture in America. When CAEL was established in 1974 under the leadership of Morris Keeton it had the following objectives:

- to develop and disseminate techniques for evaluating work and life experiences that can be given academic credit
- to create and distribute publications to help those involved with adult and experiential learning
- to expand research-based knowledge about adult learners and good practice in assessment of their prior learning.

SCOPE OF PRIOR LEARNING ASSESSMENT IN AMERICA

Knapp and Gardner (1981) and Lamdin (1991) state that in the USA assessment of prior learning, better known in America as prior learning assessment (PLA), has been developed mainly through The Council for Adult and Experiential Learning (CAEL). In 1974 CAEL, then known as The Co-operative Assessment of Experiential Learning (CAEL) sponsored a PLA project with a view to:

- understanding how experiential learning was being viewed by institutions for purposes of academic credit
- understanding how sponsored (known in UK as certificated) prior learning was being viewed by institutions for purposes of academic credit
- establishing procedures by which experiential and sponsored learning would be given credit or recognition.

The CAEL research project was supported by a consortium of institutions and became a major catalyst for systematic approach to PLA. The project also marked the beginnings of the need for a good practice guide.

Non-college credits

The greatest challenge to faculty members seemed to be the recognition of non-college credits as having any academic currency. Many faculty members (Knapp and Gardner 1981) were worried that non-college credits would be credits given on the strength of the experience as opposed to clear evidence of learning. Paradoxically, adult learners from, for instance, the armed forces, were already getting academic credit for their prior learning through:

- College Level Examination Programme (CLEP)
- American Council on Education (ACE)

College Level Examination Programme and American Council on Education's prior learning systems signalled the new phenomenon of portfolio assessment. Indeed, portfolio assessments appeared at several new breed colleges established within the liberation spirit of the sixties. Such colleges as Minnesota Metropolitan College, Empire State College and Governors State University routinely offered PLA opportunities to learners. In the light of these variable practices and developments, CAEL would, perhaps rightly, claim that their mere presence through the research and development project which was fully supported by several large institutions and well funded by federal and private foundations gave higher education a clear signal that PLA was to become a very important option for their students. To date it could be argued CAEL has had a profound influence on the development and shape of PLA both in America and elsewhere. For instance, Norman Evans, one of the early exponents of APL in the UK has had links with CAEL as far back as 1977 (Evans 1992). CAEL has had similar stories and links in many parts of the globe. In fact, in 1994 CAEL marked its twentieth anniversary with an international conference that brought together about 1,600 people from no fewer than 32 countries. In terms of promoting good practice, CAEL has several publications including Whitaker (1989), Knapp and Gardner (1981), Keeton (1976) and Education Testing Services (ETS 1987). These texts clearly articulate the need for good practice and go on to suggest standards, principles and procedures necessary for good practice. Generally, most of these standards and principles are shared, although the terminology sometimes used make this sharing less obvious.

DEVELOPMENT OF APL IN THE UK

While the preceding section has clearly suggested that the USA has greatly influenced international APL developments, it can be argued that the original idea started in the UK as far back as 1836 (Nyatanga 1993). Within the UK it may also be argued that The Open University restarted APL as far back as 1970 (also see Chapter Six) although it was only formalised in March 1986. Since the formalisation of the credit system in the UK, both APL and APEL (Assessment of Prior Experiential Learning) have become widely accepted. Just like CAEL in America, the then Council for National Academic Awards (CNAA) became a catalyst for the rapid and efficient implementation of APL and APEL. For ease of expression the term APL will hereafter be used to refer to general issues of assessment involving both certificated and uncertificated learning.

In the UK, APL appears to be an integral part of modularisation and the credit accumulation and transfer scheme (CATS). In fact, a few institutions prefer to call their schemes credit accumulation and modular schemes (CAMS) to denote the combination of modularisation and CATS. As will be seen in Chapter Six, CATS itself came about as a result of political and educational pressure to create more flexible ways of learning. This chapter will confine itself to those developments closely associated with APL. Due to space the key developments will be presented as a table (see Table 1).

Table 1 *Key developments associated with APL*

Year	Key developments
1977	CNAA and Open University agree to enable students to transfer between them with credit for past studies. Minister of State, Gordon Oakes MP, holds consultative meeting to discuss credit transfer. Steering group set up which includes CNAA's Chief Officer Dr Edwin Kerr and CDP's Chairman Dr Raymond Rickett.
1979	DES funds feasibility study of educational transfer which is directed by Mr Peter Toyne, then at Exeter University.
1981	CNAA identifies international potential of credit transfer. 'There is an urgent need to consider some system of credit transfer extending beyond the bounds of one country.'
1983	CNAA conference on CATS and the future of courses at undergraduate level. CNAA convenes a working party on credit transfer and accumulation which begins the process of considering a pilot scheme.
1984	Parliamentary Under-Secretary of State at the DES, Peter Brooke, invites the CNAA to act as a catalyst in developing a trans-binary credit transfer system.
1986	CNAA sets up CAT scheme advisory board under the chairmanship of Peter Toyne. CNAA appoints Dr Derek Pollard to direct the scheme.
1986	600 students seek help, with 200 being placed in courses by the end of September. 35 universities and 65 public sector institutions express support for the scheme. 30 local consortia of educational institutions and associated industrial or other organisations are established. More than 60 industrial and commercial concerns approach the CNAA with a view to getting their in-house training courses recognised for CNAA awards.
1987	CNAA conference looks at ways of creating a more open and flexible system of higher education in Scotland. IBM becomes the first company to have its in-house training credit rated as part of a degree course in a partnership scheme with Portsmouth Polytechnic. CNAA discussion document circulated to employers and professional associations proposing that graduates should be able to use their training and experience at work to help gain postgraduate awards.
1988	University of London signs CATS agreement with CNAA to give students the chance to accumulate a degree by building up learning credits acquired from universities, polytechnics, colleges or places of work. CNAA holds two conferences with the Standing Conference on University Entrance to encourage more universities to start CAT schemes. First meeting of Access Steering Committee, chaired by Professor Peter Toyne, Rector, Liverpool Polytechnic. DES invites CNAA to co-ordinate work in partnership with CVCP. (Access courses prepare students without the 'normal' qualifications for entry to degree courses). 500 courses are planned involving 5,000 students.
1988	Wimpy becomes the first company to apply directly to the CNAA to obtain a central credit rating for their in-house training. The first centrally registered CNAA CATS student graduates.

Table 1 *(contd.)*

Year	Key developments
1989	CNAA conference to consider the relevance of credit transfer to engineering degree and postgraduate courses.
	Teachers who successfully complete in-service courses in science education can gain credit towards undergraduate and postgraduate degrees as a result of an agreement between CNAA and the Association for Science Education.
	CNAA recognises the Forensic Science Diploma for credit in an agreement with the Forensic Science Society, the first professional body to establish a link with CATS.
	New publication sets out the arrangements for the recognition of Access courses.
	CNAA appoints first officer for Scotland, Harry Mitchell, to help develop CATS in Scottish universities and central institutions.
	CNAA gives academic credit for professional qualifications in nursing, midwifery and health visiting in an agreement with the English National Board for Nursing, Midwifery and Health Visiting.
	CNAA and CVCP invited to set up a central body for co-ordinating arrangements to provide a framework of quality assurance for Access courses.
	Directory of Access courses published.
	Seven universities sign agreement with CNAA to adopt CATS credit tariff system. (Bradford, Brunel, City, Keele, Oxford, Sheffield and Warwick.)
1990	Scottish CATS (SCOTCAT) regulations approved.
	A CNAA survey indicates that 16 polytechnics and colleges have CAT schemes already in place. A further 11 would be operational later that year and four more by September 1991. Four further institutions indicated their intention of developing CAT schemes. The CNAA had also negotiated agreements on credit transfer with 11 universities.
	16 agencies authorised to approve Access courses. (Authorised Validating Agencies.)
	BT becomes the first commercial organisation to be formally associated with the CNAA by offering in-house training leading directly to the Certificate in Management. This was the first time a nationally recognised academic course had been run entirely in-company.
1991	All eight Scottish universities join CNAA's SCOTCAT scheme.
1992	Higher Education Quality Council (HEQC) replaces CNAA.
	Harry Mitchell (Head of the then CATS & Access division of HEQC) encourages the development of SCOTCAT's APL system.
1994	HEQC publish the Robertson report 'Choosing to change' which offers a review of the current state and issues within CATS and APL.

The interdependency of CATS and APL meant that the two issues were often discussed simultaneously. Thus, in the same way that definitions of modules, notional student study hours necessary per module, nature of assessments and the number of credits per module were being debated, so was the discussion on the terminology and nature of the APL process. One of the early issues to be resolved was that of choosing a typical APL model that most institutions could work with. On the whole, the model presented below has general utility in the UK.

The model illustrated in Figure 1 embraces six distinct stages albeit variously expressed. These are pre-entry, profiling, gathering of evidence, assessment, accreditation and post-assessment guidance. The main activities suggested for each stage (Simosko 1991; Open University 1990) appear to be in keeping with the development of good practice across institutions of various histories and aspirations.

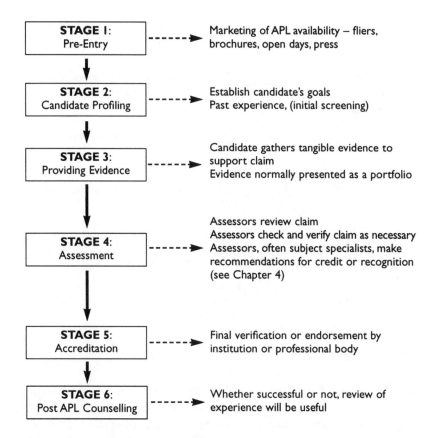

| STAGE 1:
Pre-Entry | ┄┄┄► | Marketing of APL availability – fliers,
brochures, open days, press |

STAGE 1:
Pre-Entry ┄┄┄► Marketing of APL availability – fliers, brochures, open days, press

STAGE 2:
Candidate Profiling ┄┄┄► Establish candidate's goals
Past experience, (initial screening)

STAGE 3:
Providing Evidence ┄┄┄► Candidate gathers tangible evidence to support claim
Evidence normally presented as a portfolio

STAGE 4:
Assessment ┄┄┄► Assessors review claim
Assessors check and verify claim as necessary
Assessors, often subject specialists, make recommendations for credit or recognition (see Chapter 4)

STAGE 5:
Accreditation ┄┄┄► Final verification or endorsement by institution or professional body

STAGE 6:
Post APL Counselling ┄┄┄► Whether successful or not, review of experience will be useful

Figure 1 *Example of APL model commonly used in UK*

Figure 2 shows the American version which is thought to have more similarities than differences. This is presented purely for comparison purposes.

THE DISTINCTION BETWEEN APL AND APEL

The distinction between APL and APEL remains somewhat blurred. Initially, however, APL has been associated with certificated prior learning. APL, therefore, relates to such prior learning as may be gained through organised courses, modules, workshops, seminars and similar activities. Thus, in the broad sense, APL covers two aspects of prior learning, namely (a) prior learning intentionally organised for which certification marks successful completion and (b) organised prior learning such as seminars where certification is not necessarily issued. The common aspects of APL are that they are both organised learning, or sponsored learning, as it is sometimes called in America.

APEL, on the other hand, has been associated with incidental prior learning. APEL therefore relates to such prior learning as may be gained through leisure pursuits, family experiences, and unstructured work experience. Such learning is seldom certificated,

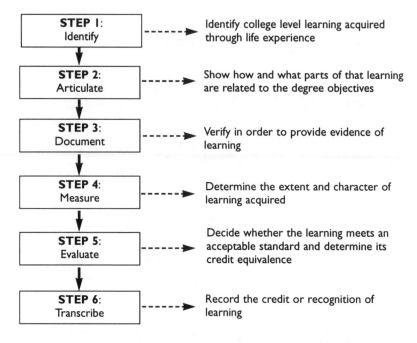

Figure 2 *The American APL model*

hence the use of 'uncertificated prior learning'. While both forms of prior learning focus on learning rather than experience, and outcome rather than process, they can differ in the way candidates may gather and submit evidence to support their claim. It is for this purpose that the distinction is important (see also Chapter 6). For instance, the APL candidates may be able to produce relevant certificates as well as syllabus or module outline in support of their claim. It is possible that a candidate seeking recognition of their prior certificated learning may do so without necessarily producing a portfolio. Alternatively, an APL candidate may produce what is sometimes known as a composite portfolio which is a brief outline of what was learnt. The outline is therefore used to expand orally through the APL interview and for the interviewers to write a summary report of how APL accords with stated learning outcomes. APEL, on the other hand, relies heavily on the production of a portfolio which should be matched to stated learning outcomes of a given programme or module.

GOOD PRACTICE SUMMARY

Any authentic practice requires that there be an agreed code of practice. APL is no different. Given the diversity of circumstances and levels of use it requires clear guides on what is to be avoided. Some of the practices to be avoided were identified during shadow visits to a number of institutions in the UK between 1990 and 1992. These may be summarised as follows:

Ten APL Malpractices to be avoided:

- Granting credits for 'time served' or just for experience.
- Basing assessment fees (Portfolio etc.) on the number of credits awarded.
- Failure to focus on specific credits and programmes.
- Failing to separate the role of APL Advisor from that of Assessor.
- Promising an APL service without regard for resources, staff development and expertise in the area.
- Having no method of checking inconsistencies and APL malpractice: offering unco-ordinated and inauthentic service.
- Failing to publicly declare in advance the rules, regulations and criteria used for APL assessment.
- Failing to provide a justified transcription of APL outcomes, including sufficiency of evidence as part of quality assurance.
- Failing to give feedback to intending students.
- Promising credits and/or admission to programme before assessment takes place. (Not checking authenticity of claim.)

Chapter 2

The Nature of Evidence

INTRODUCTION

This chapter starts from the premise that learning occurs throughout life. In appropriate cases such learning can be quantified and assessed with a view to awarding academic credit or professional recognition. To this end, the evidence that a student deserves academic credit is crucial and can take any of the following three forms:

- The student can submit relevant certificate(s) demonstrating previous learning.
- The student can undertake and pass the assessment which they would have undertaken for the credit for which they are applying.
- The student can submit a variety of evidence which is matched to the details of the syllabus/competence criteria for which they are requesting credit. This submission of evidence takes the form of what is termed a portfolio and it is the nature of this evidence that will be the main focus of this chapter.

Lamdin (1992) describes a portfolio as a formal written communication, presented to an institution/awarding body by the student requesting recognition and/or credits for previous learning.

The portfolio, Lamdin suggests, must clearly articulate the 'learning' rather than the experience and must provide tangible evidence so that assessors can use it alone or in conjunction with other evidence for the purposes of awarding credits.

PORTFOLIO NARRATIVES AND LEARNING OUTCOMES

The construction of a portfolio for most students/clients is a new and somewhat daunting process. Guidance on how to embark on the reflective process, which will ultimately lead to the production of the evidence, is a skill that needs developing. It is not surprising, therefore, that institutions concerned about quality and principles of good APL practice have established processes and mechanisms for supporting students who seek APL. As part of the discussion of the nature of evidence this chapter will therefore highlight some six basic questions considered useful for understanding the concept of portfolio.

(1) What does a portfolio consist of?
(2) How does this differ from a profile?
(3) How do you begin to construct a portfolio?
(4) How do you analyse experiential learning and produce the evidence required?
(5) How is this matched to the competencies/learning outcomes required?
(6) How are all the above factors brought together for the portfolio?

1. What does a portfolio consist of?

The content of a portfolio will differ according to the person producing it and the purpose of the portfolio. For example, the content of a portfolio which is to be assessed for an art-based programme may have examples of art work in the form of photographs or exhibition details. A portfolio for an experimental science-based programme may contain examples of experimental work that has led to significant learning. Significant here is used to also mean relevant and creditable learning. While accepting individual differences, it is strongly suggested that portfolios should, as far as practicable, adopt a common format as presented below. This affords a degree of equity and comparability akin to the structure and word limit ascribed to most module or unit assignments.

A typical portfolio layout will contain:

- a front cover with full name and address of candidate, followed by APEL or APL or APCL portfolio submission for entry with or without advanced standing. Portfolios are generally expected if a claim involves experiential learning (APEL) or a combination of experiential learning and prior certificated learning (APCL). Claims based on purely certificated or sponsored learning do not usually require a portfolio.
- date of submission and name of institution/professional body awarding credits for advanced standing must be clearly indicated followed by the following:
    - first inside page providing a contents list
    - each narrative/explanation (as above) should be presented separately and cross-referenced to relevant (matched against) programme objectives
    - evidence as appendices should be systematically matched to the narratives/explanations
    - other appropriate evidence (if not too bulky) should be clearly labelled, cross-referenced and attached
    - a clear summary of the modules or programmes claimed should be stated together with the number of credits expected.

2. How does this differ from a profile?

The term 'profiling' has often been confused with that of portfolio construction. The Open University (OU) describes the initial interviewing of an APL student as a profiling process consisting of six stages:

- welcome and introduction
- establish candidates' goals, knowledge of APL and general expectations
- reflection on previous learning
- matching previous learning to specific goals
- matching competencies with stated outcomes
- enrolment on portfolio construction/development with clear timetable and responsibilities for further action

This whole profiling process is described by Simosko (1991) as being the second part of the six stages of APL:

- pre-entry
- profiling
- collect evidence
- assessment

- accreditation
- post–assessment guidance

Profiling is a very important aspect of the APL process because it helps clarify expectations of both the student and the programme or institution. Where such expectations are incongruous, profiling can stop unnecessary waste of time otherwise incurred in proceeding with portfolio construction. Thus profiling is also a useful diagnostic tool to be used before engaging in a portfolio construction exercise. These days, profiling can be done very quickly using appropriate computer technology such as that being developed by the National Council for Educational Technology (NCET) which is also capable of assessing the whole APL claim.

3. How do you begin to construct a portfolio?

From the discussion so far it should be clear that the production of a portfolio should be for a specific award or programme of study. Each award and ideally each part of the award, or module of the programme, will have set competence criteria or learning outcomes, against which a student studying on the programme will be assessed.

If a student wishes to be given advanced standing for particular parts of the award, or modules of a programme, then the portfolio should be constructed to address the competence criteria, or learning outcomes identified. This establishes clear goals for the APL student.

An example of clear criteria which the student could be aiming towards is shown below for a GNVQ programme.

Table 2 *Performance criteria for GNVQ*

UNIT 2 – INTERPERSONAL INTERACTION LEVEL 3

Element 2.1: Communicate with individuals

Performance Criteria:

1. The method of communication is suitable to the individual needs of others.
2. Communication techniques are used to convey effective supportive skills.
3. The form of communication conveys positive value of others.
4. Factors which inhibit interpersonal interaction are explained and avoided.

Range:

- Method of communication: verbal; non-verbal
- Communication techniques: face-to-face; tone of voice; body language; oral signs (e.g. ums, ahs); reflection of own and other's behaviour; active listening and responding.
- Supportive skills: conveying warmth; conveying understanding; conveying sincerity.
- Individual needs: physical; cognitive; social emotional; behavioural.
- Positive value of others: respect for others; personal preference; choice; independence.
- Factors: distractions; dominating the conversation; manipulating; blocking others' contributions; culturally dependent behaviour.

Evidence Indicators:

Explanation and analysis of communication with two individuals with contrasting needs, to include an individual with a communication disability. Evidence should demonstrate an understanding of the implications of the range of dimensions in relation to the element. Evidence which a student/client may produce for these criteria will be considered in more depth in Chapter 7 (Part Two of this book).

4. How do you analyse experiential learning and produce the evidence required?

First, let's consider the nature of the evidence which may be available or could be produced.

Nature of evidence

A further criterion which should be borne in mind is the assessment methods by which the student and their portfolio will be judged.

Nyatanga and Fox (1993), in describing the nature of evidence, list five methods of assessment, namely:

- written tests
- demonstration/simulation
- assignments
- viva voce
- product evaluation.

However, there are other forms of evidence and perhaps it would be helpful to consider them in terms of direct and indirect evidence.

Direct and indirect evidence

Direct evidence, or primary evidence as it is often called is the evidence that reflects the student or applicant's own work such as previous reports, publications, and so on. These can take the form of:

- monthly or annual written reports
- written internal correspondence
- spreadsheets of financial data
- videos of presentations
- schematic diagrams of changes to interior fixtures
- graphs indicating analysed data
- staffing schedules
- audio recordings of meetings
- copies of published articles
- computerised software data.

The list is endless and as indicated above can take a variety of forms. However, even if it were not possible to produce any of the above, an assessor or colleague could observe a 'performance' and this too may be used as evidence, providing of course the 'observer' is suitably qualified to form a judgement, or can act as a witness.

Indirect evidence is in contrast to that which is collected from others about you. The most common of these to be found in a portfolio are:

- Minutes of meetings
- Witness testimonies.

The example of 'minutes of meetings' is self explanatory, however 'witness testimonies' require a little more explanation. More examples and their application are given in Part Two.

A witness testimony is written in two parts:

Part A provides guidance for the witness in responding to requests in that they should:

i) Check whether the awarding body (e.g. College, City & Guilds, etc.) with which the student is registered offers guidance notes.

ii) If so, follow these as far as possible but they may also wish to cross-refer to the following points:
- check the title of the award or part of the award for which the student requires the witness testimony.
- obtain a copy of the learning outcomes or competence criteria from the student.
- ask the student to outline the occasions/circumstances on which they are expected to report.
- obtain written agreement from the student to waive the right to use or disclose their testimony for any purpose other than as evidence for the learning outcome or competence statements specified.

The testimony should be written by them in a personal capacity based on their personal knowledge of the student.

Part B offers advice on the formulation of the Witness Testimony as follows:

i) As a witness you are not expected to be familiar with all the details and nuances of the learning outcomes or competencies; these are the assessors' concerns. Likewise you are not expected to make judgements about the way in which the student has acted.

ii) As a witness you are required to describe in factual terms how the candidate acted in particular circumstances using the learning outcomes or competence criteria as your guide.

iii) Try to avoid making value judgements e.g. 'she behaved wonderfully to bring the situation under control'. Your aim is to describe what the candidate did in an objective way so that the assessor appreciates what was achieved, e.g. 'participants were getting angry so she suggested that we take a coffee break and spoke to the two who were most heated and persuaded them to agree a compromise'.

iv) Always remember to state your relationship to the student and include the date/duration of the event/circumstance on which you are reporting.

The MCI (1992) state that a witness testimony should contain:

- company heading; name of supervisor or manager
- period of employment
- list of competencies
- statement of verification
- signature and position of person verifying the claim
- the date

and also offers guidance to providers of witness testimonies. The following section could be done as a letter to the provider of the testimony.

Table 3 *Guidance to providers of testimony*

GUIDANCE TO PROVIDERS OF A WITNESS TESTIMONY

You are being asked to write on behalf of a manager or supervisor who is seeking recognition, credit and/or qualifications for competencies he/she already has. If you have agreed to write on behalf of this manager or supervisor, we would appreciate you following these guidelines:

1. Please make sure that your letter or report is on company/business letterhead paper and typed, if at all possible.
2. Include in your letter or report:
   a. the manager or supervisor's name
   b. dates of employment (or time during which you knew or worked with the supervisor or manager)
   c. post(s) held by the manager or supervisor and the capacity in which you know/knew him/her
   d. a list of the competencies which the supervisor or manager is claiming (as described in the MCI Crediting Competence Framework)
   e. a statement of your verification (if you agree) and a summary description of the context in which the competencies have been demonstrated
   f. your signature and position.

Please note the Witness testimonies may not be used as the sole source of information to assess the manager's or supervisor's competence, however, they are often used in conjunction with other types of evidence and can play an important role in the supervisor's or manager's assessment. For this reason, please do not testify to any claim in which you feel the applicant is not fully competent.

If done as a letter then the usual closing remarks may include 'Thank you for your time' or other appropriate remark.Other forms of indirect evidence which may be included in your portfolio are:

- appraisals of you undertaken by others
- newspaper cuttings about you
- prizes or certificates
- references given about you
- photographs of you undertaking a role
- simulations of the role.

When thinking of using any direct or indirect evidence, careful consideration needs to be given to ensure that it is matched to the learning outcomes or assessment criteria against which it is to be assessed. Often an explanation or report is required which can:

- enable the assessor to put the evidence into context by describing some of the background to the organisation or circumstances which gave rise to the evidence;
- clarify the relationship of the evidence to the learning outcomes or competencies, in terms of the underlying theory used in deriving the evidence.

Reflection in this way has the added benefit of enabling the individual to acknowledge what they have learned and perhaps consider how they will undertake similar tasks in the future, all of which is of course a very valuable part of the learning process.

Perhaps some helpful questions in thinking about the evidence which is to be collected are:

* Is there anything which I already have?
* Do I produce any evidence on a regular basis?
* Can I modify my actions so that direct or indirect evidence can be easily achieved?
* Can I obtain evidence from past or current colleagues?

Now we can understand the nature of the evidence we should be producing, let's look at how this is matched to the learning outcomes or competencies.

5. How is this matched to the competencies/learning outcomes required?

Examples of matching evidence to competencies and learning outcomes can be found in Chapters 7 and 8. The NVQ and MCI systems demand that performance criteria and range statements are adhered to as well as competencies, whereas with learning outcomes a little more flexibility is possible.

Distinction between a claim and evidence

From time to time claimants may exaggerate what has been achieved. This may be due to a variety of reasons that will not be pursued here. However, anyone constructing a portfolio should bear in mind the key criteria which the assessor will be using to judge the portfolio. This will help link appropriate evidence to each of the criteria and thereby reduce unnecessary exaggeration.

Key quality criteria which the assessor is looking for

For each candidate the assessors should observe principles of validity, reliability, sufficiency, authenticity and relevance/currency.
   A brief description of each is given below:

* validity: that the assessment identifies knowledge and skills it purports to assess
* reliability: that the assessment can be repeated with the same outcome
* sufficiency: that the assessor knows and judges the appropriateness, comprehensiveness and quality of evidence
* authenticity: that it is the applicant's own learning being given credit
* currency: that the evidence presented is relevant to the purpose of the portfolio. In other words the evidence must satisfy the stated learning outcomes. The argument of shelf life per se is irrelevant. What really matters is the relevance of past learning to the objectives or outcomes in question.

6. How are all the above factors brought together for the portfolio?

The role of the advisor and the assessor

The APL advisor for MCI is usually a person who is specifically trained and accredited to help in the process of development, and in the compilation of evidence for assessment.

The liaison between the advisor and the assessor

Further details about the assessment process can be found in Chapter 6, but it is helpful here to discuss the distinction between the advisor and assessor roles.

The role of the APL advisor The role of the APL advisor throughout the process is that of facilitator. The advisor can be a generalist as opposed to a subject specialist although current practice tends to suggest the advisor also needs to be a subject specialist. The facilitator role can be summarised as follows:

a) initial screening or profiling
b) ensuring the candidate understands the APL guiding principles
c) advise on pathways open to candidates
d) advise on general portfolio construction process and nature of evidence
e) advise candidate on relevance/currency and sufficiency of claim
f) facilitate the development of self confidence during the process
g) when portfolio is ready for submission sign submission form.

The role of the assessors
Making an assessment is not easy!

> Pilot error causing a crash suggests that had the assessment process been more thorough a weakness in competence, perhaps associated with carrying out routine tasks in stressful conditions such as flying in fog, may have been identified. And at the other end of the spectrum we all know of examples where the apparently 'competent' have surprised us. The fact is that it is impossible to arrive at judgements about most human activities which are 100% certain. Actually such precision is rarely required.

The assessors are, however, custodians of academic/professional standards and quality. They have to evaluate the evidence against programme learning outcomes or competence criteria. They are at the same time trying to mediate between the individual's idiosyncratic language and perceptions of their previous learning.

As previously stated, assessment is not easy!

Perhaps before we look at the considerations to be taken by the assessor with regard to the portfolio we should first consider the efficiency with which we are going to undertake the assessment process. Such considerations include:

• How much training are we going to allow the assessor?
• How much time is going to be made available for the assessor to carry out the assessment?
• What types of assessment material are we expecting the assessor to deal with?
• Has the assessor sufficient background knowledge of the area to carry out the assessment?
• Are we prepared to cross check the assessment has been carried out correctly/consistently/comparably with other assessors?
• Will an external examiner/verifier check the assessment?

In short are we sure the assessor is competent?

Quality and the assessment process

Ensuring good practice in the assessment process means:

- choosing an assessor who has the appropriate background knowledge to carry out the assessment
- allowing the assessor the training, time and tools appropriate to undertaking the role
- clarifying the criteria on which the assessment will be based
- checking that comparisons between assessors are undertaken
- verifying the decisions taken by allowing an external examiner to sample the assessments made.

Additionally, encouraging or utilising the advice and guidance from external verifiers and fostering a perception of quality assurance as an ongoing process which has both formative and summative assessment throughout the year will ensure quality assurance issues have a prominent focus.

In the UK institutions, recommending specific credits implies further judgements:

- number of credits
- an academic level of those recommended credits.

If all else fails it may help to remember the following quote:

> Making an assessment of competence is like making a judgement about most human activities. In some cases we feel absolutely certain that the individual can do something, in other cases we are 'pretty certain', we can be uncertain, and we can be absolutely certain that they cannot do it.

GOOD PRACTICE SUMMARY

There are about seven guiding principles that have been incorporated into good practice in APL.

Principle 1: The student/candidate should make the claim

For APL the most important guiding principle throughout is that it is the student or applicant who makes the claim. It follows that the responsibility rests with the student for making a claim and supporting the claim with appropriate evidence. In many applications students need considerable help in preparing evidence and in understanding what might be a sensible claim to make, but it is vital to recognise where the prime responsibility lies.

Principle 2: APL is about learning outcomes, not just experience

The insistence throughout must be that the experience of a student is significant only as a source of learning. The intellectual task of moving from a description of experience to an identification of the learning derived from that experience is demanding. But if it cannot be accomplished there is no learning to assess, however important to the individual that experience may have been.

Principle 3: Identification of significant learning should come before assessment

A third guiding principle is that there is a clear separation between the identification of prior learning and organising it into forms fit for presenting for assessment, and the assessment itself. The identification of prior learning comes through systematic reflection on experience and there are four stages within that:

1. Systematic reflection on past experience
2. Identification of significant learning
3. Synthesis of evidence through portfolio
4. Evaluation by assessors.

Principle 4: Assessment is an academic responsibility

Academic assessment is solely the responsibility of staff approved by the awarding academic institution. It is open to staff to employ any procedure they think appropriate to arrive at an academic judgement about the evidence of prior learning submitted. Normally, good practice requires that a submitted portfolio be assessed by at least two assessors. The assessors should not have been actively involved as counsellors or advisors during the portfolio construction phase (see Principle 6).

Principle 5: Evidence must be appropriate

The fifth guiding principle concerns the nature of evidence submitted for assessment. As with all academic assessments, the method of assessment needs to be appropriate for what is being assessed. Hence, in conjunction with the portfolio submitted, academic staff may choose to request a variety of further evidence to support the student's claim. As a result they may decide to probe a student's level of knowledge through an interview either in person or by telephone. They may require additional written or assignment work. They may examine artefacts or observe performance. Whatever method of assessment is used, it must be such that the judgement made can be considered by external examiners and boards of examiners alongside and with the same degree of confidence as other more traditionally assessed performances such as formal examination results.

Principle 6: Two academic functions (advocate vs judge) should be separated

As a general rule and as a sixth guiding principle, it is wise to separate the two academic functions of helping students prepare evidence of learning and assessing that learning. In other words, staff who help students prepare evidence should not have any direct role in making the final academic judgements about that evidence.

The above six principles are based on the initial work of Evans (1988).

Principle 7: Quality should be assured within the APL process

This principle seeks to ensure that admission tutors, subject assessment teams/boards are satisfied that:

- the portfolio or other evidence has been conclusive
- the number and level of credits to be awarded has been identified and agreed
- written feedback is given to the applicant within six weeks of submitting a portfolio.

Chapter 3

The Assessment and Accreditation Process

INTRODUCTION

Theories and methodological debates concerning assessment have abounded for many years, not only in the United Kingdom but also in other industrialised countries and more lately the developing world. The debate often seeks to explore complementary yet also independent aspects of the complex notion of assessment. Some debates adopt a psychological or sociological perspective seeking to explore the effect of assessment upon motivational focus or dynamics of learning. Other forms of debates have given emphasis to the 'best' approaches in assessment in terms of enhancing the assessment validity and authenticity, for example oral modes of assessment, problem solving/simulation strategy or practical work. Equally, debates about assessment have adopted a more macro perspective in terms of issues of compatibility of standards and the use of assessment outcomes as audit of organisations efficiency and value for money. In the midst of such debates educators have sought to be increasingly open about the aims, strategies, regulations and standards of assessment pertinent to each educational programme; together with those germane to the educational institution as a whole.

Programmes generally use learning outcomes that carry assumptions about valued knowledge. In most cases these learning outcomes continue to reflect the traditional and philosophical views (Ryle 1949) of *knowing that* factual knowledge and *knowing how* practical or procedural knowledge. From this perspective it is easy to see how the various forms of assessments (Gipps and Stobart 1993; Dixon 1993) continue to assess these two forms of knowledge. It logically follows that APL also assesses these two forms of knowledge.

Assessment of competencies (knowing how)

> Ten years ago competency based assessment, to most people who had heard of it (if at all), was a rather laissez-faire approach associated with reform movements in American teacher education. Today it occupies a central place in British education and training and is the subject of large-scale government support
>
> Wolf (1995)

In many instances APL is associated with such competency-based learning; in that it gives credit for existing competencies. By so doing it avoids duplication of learning and encourages progression. Wolf (1995, p. 115) reaffirms this view in discussion of the relationship between APL and competency-based NVQ learning:

> a guiding principle of the NVQ framework has always been that people should gain credit for displayed competence, however they acquire it. Qualifications should not be tied to training programmes, time spent in education or 'time served' in apprenticeship, given to the process by which previously acquired competence can be displayed and credited.

The assessment of achievement or competencies in a process of APL, Quinn (1994) suggests, has served, to challenge the established canons of education in terms of the curriculum design. This includes educational programmes and related curriculum models and the role of the teacher/educator. Achievement of competencies (knowing how) places an emphasis upon process-based curriculum rather than product-based. In this context, Quinn suggests the role of assessment in a process curriculum is very different from that in a product one in that the assessor may also act as a critical appraiser in a formative way. Thus the teacher or advisor is cast in the role of critical appraiser of the student's work and at the same time the student is learning and developing critical self-appraisal skills. Quinn's position appears to be congruent with the earlier work by Beattie (1987), who saw the curriculum as a portfolio of meaningful personal experiences, within which the student is placed at the centre of the process.

Nevertheless, while the relationship between competency-based learning and APL is generally accepted, it still remains a source of debate; including the nature of assessment within this. This is ideally illustrated by Butterworth (1992) who debates a distinction between competency-based APL in general and its more specific form in terms of professional development. He suggests that in its generic form the emphasis of assessment is upon the production by the claimant of evidence of past achievements, while in its professional form (for example as used by nurses) there is an additional requirement to analyse such evidence as to its significance for professional development.

In summary, therefore, it is helpful to acknowledge that APL is capable of adequately assessing and valuing competency-based activities (knowing how) as well as cognitive-based activities (knowing that).

VALIDITY AND RELIABILITY OF APL ASSESSMENTS

It is perhaps helpful first to explore the notions of validity/reliability within assessment processes in a general way before consideration of the specific application of this to APL. One of the first questions in considering assessment is: what are we testing and can we be sure it is what we wish to test (validity)? This is closely followed by a second question: can we be sure that the assessment will test in the same way on more than one occasion or to more than one individual, in other words consistency (or reliability)? Traditionally, educators have developed a vast array of assessment strategies and testing tools in an attempt to obtain the elusive goal of validity and reliability, albeit often implicitly.

For each programme or award, this elusive goal is often achieved by internal marking arrangements. In some cases this involves double marking, use of external examiners or equivalent, and assessment boards. A great deal of importance is rightly placed on the role and function of external examiners or external verifiers/moderators because they are considered to be disinterested. The fact that there is a difference in both meaning and role function between external examiners and verifiers, and that institutions have different expectations, will not be pursued here. The point is that the involvement of all these people in the assessment of student work is intended to enhance validity and reliability as well as overall quality. Readers familiar with APL assessment will immediately recognise the above arrangements as being also true of APL, and in most cases more so than in conventional assessments. Readers familiar with APL will also know that it is not the cheap option often suggested by ill-informed critics of APL. Rather, it is an approach that has challenged our understanding of academic levels and their related assessments (see also Chapter 6).

Evans (1992, p. 6) has further suggested that validity of APL may be enhanced by ensuring that assessment is undertaken by two assessors and 'through assimilating assessments of prior learning to the normal internal academic procedures for examining laid out as requirements for conduct of the degree course.'

Additionally, APL assessments require the following expanded checklist to enhance the development of good practice.

APL assessment: good practice checklist

- Validity: that the assessment does identify the correct knowledge or skills to be assessed.
- Reliability: that the assessment be trusted to produce the same or similar outcomes all the time.
- Sufficiency: that we know or can judge the appropriateness of evidence.
- Authenticity: that it is the applicants own learning for which credit is being sought.
- Relevance: that the learning to be accredited presents up-to-date knowledge and skills in relation to the intended area of study. As stated in Chapter 2 this is not an argument for shelf life per se.
- Directness: that the focus of the learning is sharp rather than diffuse. In the UK this is particularly important, because specific as opposed to general credits are often awarded.
- Breadth: that the learning covers the scope under consideration.
- Quality: that the learning has reached an acceptable level or standard.

In his discussion of validity within APL assessments, Evans continues to highlight an issue of frequent concern and debate, namely the comparability between different academic disciplines, for example engineering and sociology, each of which may have different assessment values or traditions. He suggests that some disciplines are more amenable to making judgements in which the evidence is more course related while in others the judgement essentially relates to 'conceptual group and understanding rather than in relation to content coverage and that then is the basis of their assessment' (Evans 1992, p. 89).

The key issue, therefore, that emerges in this debate is that of relevancy. Relevancy of the candidate's answer within an examination question is a relatively simple issue within traditional assessment, but rather more complex within the context of APL, in which the candidate may present a diverse range of evidence. Within APL, however, it does remain the responsibility of the candidate to demonstrate the relevancy of his/her learning in a manner that is clear and overt to the assessor. Largely, this is achieved by the quality of narrative within the portfolio and system of referencing of the evidence against the elements of competence or learning outcomes.

The notion of validity within APL does, however, acquire a particular perspective in which it becomes incumbent upon the assessor to check the validity of the evidence presented. In other words to determine whether a candidate's claim is genuine – while observation as a mode of assessment if undertaken directly by the APL assessor is indisputable.

For example:

- Written evidence may have been produced by an individual other than the candidate and may therefore be checked by oral questioning.
- Supportive letters may not be genuine and may require attention in terms of ensuring they are written on an appropriate organisational 'headed paper' and a telephone call of verification to the author.

In this context McKelvey and Peters (1993) offer some helpful prompts.

- Does the evidence match in part or wholly the competencies set down in the performance criteria?
- Can it be believed?
- Has it been questioned?
- Has it been validated?
- Is it reliable?
- Is it practicable? (p. 24)

OTHER ASSESSMENT CRITERIA

One dimension to ensure a consistency of approach in assessing APL is to assess against identified criteria. As Challis (1993) has remarked, APL is not designed as other assessments are to achieve a pass or fail; it does, nevertheless, draw upon the notion of criteria referenced assessments. With respect to the value of such criteria, Gipps and Stobart (1993) have suggested that criteria referenced assessments 'are designed to reflect whether or not a student can do a specific task or range of tasks, rather than to measure how much better or worse his/her performance is in relation to that of other students' (p. 32).

Wolf (1995) also supports the view that APL assessment was born out of the ethos of criteria-referenced assessment, but also suggests that this might be more closely defined against the derivative of criteria referencing called competence-based assessment. The key characteristics of competence referencing Wolf suggests are:

1. The emphasis on outcomes – specifically, multiple outcomes, each distinctive and separately considered.
2. The belief that these can and should be specified to the point where they are clear and transparent – that assessors and third parties should be able to understand what is being assessed and what should be achieved.
3. The decoupling of assessment from particular institutions and learning programmes.

Experience has shown that clear articulation of such criteria remains a complex and challenging task for programme teams. This is particularly true when the intending APL candidate wants specific criteria and learning outcomes for the different academic levels (see also Figure 5).

Accordingly, it is perhaps not surprising to identify within the literature a number of charts, descriptors or taxonomies designed to aid the generation of criteria and the academic judgement inherent within the assessment.

An example developed as early as 1964 by Krathwohl *et al.* is given in Table 4.

Table 4 *Educational taxonomy and assessment of learning*

Generic knowledge and skills			Bloom	Krathwohl	Simpson
Data	**People**	**Other activities**	**Cognitive domain**	**Affective domain**	**Psychomotor domain**
Synthesising	Mentoring	Controlling	Evaluating	Characterisation	Organisation
Co-ordinating	Negotiating	Operating	Synthesising	Organisation	Adaptation
Analysing	Supervising	Manipulating	Analysing	Valuing	Complex overt response mechanism
Compiling	Consulting	Setting up	Responding	Responding	Guided response set
Copying	Exchanging	Tending	Receiving	Receiving	Perception
Comparing	Serving	Handling			

Based on Krathwohl, D., Bloom, B. & Masia, B. B. (1964). *Taxonomy of Educational Goals: Handbook ii: Affective Domain.* New York: Longman.

Towards a taxonomy of work-based learning in higher education

With all relatively unfamiliar activities, there is often a need to clarify and classify terms and models. Here, a provisional attempt to provide a taxonomy of approaches to WBL in order to help us understand how different focuses on the subject imply different learning opportunities for students.

WBL as Professional Practice

The work-based activity is an integral part of the education (training) programme and will cover not just the clinical practice of medical and allied professions but also the professional placements. The 'work' will normally be assessed, usually judgemental but sometimes against more objective criteria. The development of NVQs in these areas will raise interesting issues.

WBL as Sandwich Course Placement

Particularly common for programmes within the 'new' universities, the work placement generally forms part of the unassessed programme. Sandwich courses developed traditionally in those vocationally related areas where graduates from the then polytechnics were held to have been at a labour market disadvantage with graduates from the universities. The work placement was held to equalise the attractiveness to employers of polytechnic students. Recently moves have been made to accredit the work experience.

WBL as Employment-based Learning

A relatively recent development, employment-based learning might be defined as learning derived from in-company training programmes, accredited separately or in conjunction with institutionally based academic programmes, or customised programmes for discrete groups of employees, perhaps delivered on-site and defined by specific employer training needs. A good example would be the well-known scheme between the Woolwich Building Society and the University of Greenwich.

WBL as Integrated Internship

This involves the very new process where work-based internships can be developed by students as part of their main academic programme. Such internships may vary in duration but will perhaps involve a triangular negotiation on learning achievements between student, employer mentor and academic tutor. Such work-based internships may, or may not, be taken up in occupational areas related to the principal focus of the academic course. The purpose of the exercise for the student is to provide work-based academic learning as a consequence of the work experience itself, irrespective of the type or location of the work. The outcomes of the work-based learning are defined, assessed and counted towards academic awards.

This taxonomy is worthy of note in that it seeks to incorporate a range of previous theories and to embrace not only factual knowledge but also skills and values. Robertson (1992), on the other hand, explores the issue from a rather different perspective, namely approaches to work-based learning were developed into a taxonomy. Other authors (Glen and Hight 1992; Nyatanga 1991; Faltermeyer 1994) have alternatively taken specific educational taxonomies of learning and general learning theories and modified these against the need of APL. More recently Greatorex and Nyatanga (1994) have presented initial findings from a Delphi research study to elucidate the concept of academic levels in higher education in relation to APL portfolio assessment. Based on this work Nyatanga and Forman (1997) have offered a clear summary of how academic levels may be used in APL.

Without such clearly defined criteria or measures, the fears about portfolio and APL assessment identified in research undertaken by Mitchell (1994) will remain: 'Tutors also felt the portfolio was difficult to assess and expressed concerns about the subjective nature of this form of assessment.'

Clearly, if the development criteria alone are insufficient, the assessor of the portfolio will need specific staff development opportunities in order to equip him/her with the necessary knowledge, skills or confidence to undertake the assessment. The case for such specific preparation of the APL assessor is over and above the routine education any educator receives in principles and practice of assessment is made by Challis (1993): 'An APEL portfolio brings a wide range of evidence to be assessed drawn from all walks of life. Assessors have to make judgements about stated outcomes generated in areas in which they personally may have no experience and relate these to the standard performance criteria' (p. 71). The preparation of APL assessors therefore has to be seen as a priority within an organisation's staff development and training plan (see also Chapter 4).

Frequently, such preparation is given via workshops shadowing opportunities against experienced assessors, or in a more structured form via the Training and Development Lead Body Unit 36, designed specifically to develop an individual's competence in APL assessment.

STANDARDS AND ASSESSMENT

Apart from assessment achieving a given outcome for an APL applicant, it might be seen as having a secondary yet vital function in terms of setting or maintaining academic standards. In this context standards are perceived, Gipps and Stobart (1993) have suggested, as a social phenomenon; a notion of educational attainment held by the population at large. In this context therefore the notion is somewhat tenuous and certainly ill-defined; nevertheless, the assessor here is seen as the guardian of educational values and attainment on behalf of society at large and therefore does have an inevitable link to the concept of quality assurance (see Chapter 4). This aspect of assessment was part of a debate by Cohen and Whitaker (1994) in which the need to assess within a clear defensible and equitable system was highlighted. In other words, for APL to become widely accepted and valued its assessment process and outcomes need to be 'transparent' to the public at large so that assessment via APL is perceived to have reached the same standard as assessment by any other more traditional mode.

In support of this, the administrative systems are important, particularly a further checking system upon the assessment via an internal and external verifier. The primary role of verifiers is to be responsible for the monitoring and evaluation of the process and outcome of APL assessment. In so doing verifiers also affirm that assessment standards are being maintained. It is therefore important that the respective roles of the assessor and verifier are clearly delineated.

THE APL ASSESSMENT PANEL

The assessment of the portfolio may take place within the context of a formal setting or, more commonly, two named individuals will separately view the documentation and subsequently consult to form a view. The decision should be further supported by an opportunity to interview the APL applicant. This meeting and interview will provide an opportunity for the assessors to further explore or clarify elements within the portfolio and, more importantly, to satisfy themselves on behalf of the institution that issues such as authenticity and currency have been met.

The business of the 'panel', therefore, is to assess the evidence provided against the given criteria. In undertaking this some key questions might be considered:

1. Does the candidate's application address all of the outcomes/competencies; or is it sufficient that a number of them are addressed insofar as a range of relevant knowledge is demonstrated?
2. In support of a claim against a given outcome or competence, is there more than one piece of supporting evidence sufficient to substantiate the range of knowledge ability to apply such knowledge to more than one situation and clear indication that such knowledge is current?
3. Is the knowledge demonstrated at an appropriate academic level for the credit being sought?
4. Is the portfolio constructed in such a manner (see Chapter 2) as to allow the assessor to readily locate appropriate evidence, e.g. via a cross-reference system?

THE INTERVIEW

In exploring these issues as indicated the APL interview may be a helpful arena in which to clarify and confirm elements of the applicant's claim.

Fundamental to such an interview is the interviewer's expertise in interactive skills and questioning techniques appropriate for clarifying the evidence.

Guidelines for the preparation of such interviews have been produced by a number of organisations as internal documents to aid consistency of approach and hence to ensure quality. One such organisation is the College of Lifelong Learning, University of New Life, Hampshire (USA): an extract from their document 'Guidelines for faculty evaluators' is reproduced as Appendix 1.

Clearly it is important that appropriate records are made by the assessors, not only of the assessment outcome, but also of the process. Such documentation provides a valuable database for the appointed external verifier, for ongoing quality assurance/audit purposes, for future staff development activities and, most importantly, for feedback to the applicant.

FEEDBACK PROCESS

Feedback to the applicant is an important part of the APL process and is usually described in terms of communication channels, etc. within the organisation. APL policies will:

1. Indicate the outcome in terms of total credit and level.
2. (If (1) fails to match the student's claim) normally give advice as to those elements within the portfolio that might be further developed or against which additional evidence might be produced. The important dimension of feedback throughout is that assessment within APL is not a pass or fail situation, rather it is a judgement upon the evidence produced thus far.

(An illustrative example of feedback documentation is given in Chapter 8.) Accordingly, the written and supportive verbal feedback should overtly contain a section which indicates areas for further study and/or aspects for further development within the portfolio.

GOOD PRACTICE SUMMARY

From this chapter a summary of good practice can therefore be made to reflect three main areas:

1. The clarity of portfolio evidence
    – Learning outcomes or competencies must be clearly stated because portfolio evidence is normally as good as the learning outcomes they seek to fulfil.
    – The communication and advice given to the student is often reflected in the clarity of the portfolio evidence subsequently submitted.
2. Clarity of roles, especially the assessor's role
    – Ensure adequate preparation and clarification of assessor's role. Where possible, assessors must be approved by agreed methods to ensure fairness and standards.
    – Verifiers, moderators or external examiners must be appointed according to agreed criteria.

3. Clarity of the overall institutional quality assurance for APL
    - Adherence to organisational policy and regulatory framework for APL.
    - Having clear procedures for processing each application (see also Chapter 4).
    - Having clear mechanisms for monitoring and evaluating APL experiences.

Quality Assurance in APL

INTRODUCTION

Within APL, quality assurance is a term that can be used to mean the degree of confidence that students and partner agencies have in relation to perceived practice. The word 'perceived' is used to imply that quality is a social construct which, according to Koch (1992), portrays beliefs and views of worth. Generally, the concept of quality assurance is a nebulous one and the fact that there are so many terms used to describe it does not always help. For the purposes of this chapter, quality assurance will embrace aspects of total quality management (TQM) and continuous quality improvement (CQI). Deming (1986), who is considered by many to be the originator of the quality movement, sees TQM as 'doing the right thing right the first time, on time and to strive always for improvement and customer satisfaction'. For APL, 'doing it right' means having in place the infrastructure and processes for the maintenance and continuous improvement of APL practice. Thus successful APL quality assurance systems will involve institutional commitment and wider participation by significant others. Since APL is often closely related to institutional goals and programmes it should without a doubt support the institutional mission and the quality assurance mechanisms of the programmes that help fulfil that mission. For APL to complement the quality of programmes and related student experiences, it must be based on clear policy, clear commitment and critical appraisal by the users.

Most institutions have already developed such policies and procedures and infrastructures capable of assuring quality and standards. Some of these procedures involve:

- institutional policy and APL frame regulatory framework
- institutional self-evaluation (including critical peer review)
- institutional audit of artefacts
- students' feedback
- external views (may include professional bodies, external examiners and funding bodies) as part of external audit.

These elements of quality are often there to reassure programmes and institutions that the standards of their own awards are not only maintained but compare favourably with other similar institutions. To this end, the then Council for National Academic Awards (CNAA) recommended the setting up of internal audits. The academic Audit Unit of the Committee for Vice Chancellors and Principals (CVCP), now better known as the Higher Education Quality Council (HEQC)'s Division of Quality Audit (DQA), initiated a nationwide system of external audits guided by the following simple questions:

- what are you trying to do?
- why are you trying to do it?

- how are you doing it?
- why are you doing it that way?
- why do you think that is the best way of doing it?
- how do you know it works?
- how do you improve it?

(HEQC 1994)

The above questions seem central to all the issues of quality as applied to the enterprise of education. It is also clear that the above questions can inform any debate on the formulation of APL policy for any institution.

As stated in Chapter 1, the advent of modularisation, credit accumulation and transfer scheme (CATS) and accreditation of prior and experiential learning APEL in March 1986, also meant that clearer and publicly declared quality assurance processes would be imperative across all participating institutions. Inherent in any CATS provision is the acceptance of:

- flexible learning
- flexible speed of learning
- flexible mode of delivery
- quality of assessment criteria
- quality of procedures for credit rating within and across modules/programmes
- transparency of academic and administrative practices across institutions

The above issues were further complicated by the simultaneous focus and development of:

- off-campus learning or work-based learning (WBL)
- rapid developments in multimedia teaching and learning (MTL)
- developments in vocationally oriented knowledge and skills as depicted by General National Vocational Qualifications and National Vocational Qualifications (GNVQ and NVQ respectively)
- franchise arrangements between institutions
- involvement of European and overseas countries in modularisation and CATS

It is clear that these issues albeit generic to quality assurance within institutions, have direct relevance for good practice in APL. The main issues for admissions at the different stages of named programmes are:

- ensuring equality of access and opportunity for students
- ensuring that students admitted to modules and programmes on the strength of their prior learning have the potential to fulfil the learning outcomes of the programme
- that the evidence of prior learning submitted by a student is relevant to the outcomes of the intended programme
- that the institution itself has the resources and expertise that can reasonably be expected from a quality institution
- that the APL procedures and processes are rigorous as well as facilitatory.

INSTITUTIONAL MODEL FOR QUALITY ASSURANCE IN APL

It is hard to envisage how institutions can guarantee good practice and the quality of their

APL practice without taking account of:

- institutional policy specific to APL or accessibility
- agreed regulatory framework to guide both staff and students
- specific offices charged with the responsibility for the operationalisation of APL, including the monitoring of quality
- specific roles the institution and its staff will take in relation to the day-to-day APL issues
- how the institution and its programmes will be informed by external views, including views and experiences of relevant professional bodies
- how the institution will seek and integrate views and experiences of students and others involved in the APL process.

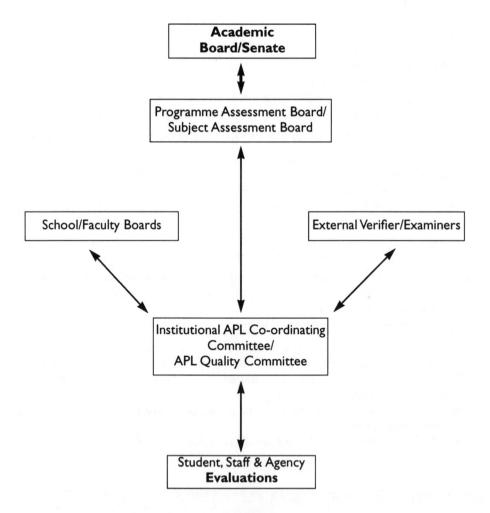

Figure 3 *Quality assurance and APL: schematic diagram*

Quality assurance issues from Figure 3

Assuming the institution has an agreed APL policy that has also been translated into appropriate resources, then the key issue becomes that of implementing the policy and related good practice. In most institutions it could be argued that the academic board or its equivalent will normally be charged with the ultimate quality assurance role for APL. If the academic board is going to succeed in its APL role it has to ensure the institution is prepared and resourced enough to meet the changing demands of APL students. The main change could be that a significant number of students will require assessment on demand services. At institutional level assessment on demand service means establishing:

- an APL assessment centre or an education shop where potential students can make enquiries about educational provisions
- an accessible APL centre staffed by well trained individuals capable of offering appropriate advice and a diagnostic APL service
- an APL database capable of speeding information about comparability and transparency of credits within and outside of subject areas. This provision would also form the basis of building individual student pathways after initial diagnosis is reached. It would additionally also form the basis for referring the potential student to appropriate subject experts who would normally carry out the final assessment.

The APL assessment centre or education centre is argued as a vital resource as it can fulfil institutional mission statements related to accessibility, equality of opportunity and maintenance of quality service. For the individual potential student the centre would offer:

- a starting point on the way to academic self-actualisation and personal fulfilment
- a clearer understanding of how individuals can quantify their previous learning for purposes of gaining academic credit
- an initial awareness, especially for adult learners, of educational culture and possible learning methods.

It is recognised the centre may also offer other services such as assessment of progress made on particular programmes of study, as well as co-ordination of other APL activities across the institution. This, of course, will depend on the size of the centre and the expertise within it.

QUALITY OF SUBJECT AND PROGRAMME ASSESSMENT

The quality assurance stated above through the establishment of an assessment or education centre is global and institutional. For the purposes of this chapter this will be known as micro quality. Thus APL micro quality should account for the following:

- Subject team perceptions and beliefs about their APL publicity material.
- Subject team perceptions of institutional mission statement in relation to APL.
- Subject team preparation and expertise in guiding potential APL students.
- Subject team in particular APL advisors' awareness of the APL guiding principles.
- Perceived quality of support and guidance during portfolio construction.

- Individual's understanding of the APL regulatory framework and related quality assurance mechanisms.
- Subject team expertise in assessing portfolios against pre-disclosed criteria and learning outcomes.
- Staff's awareness of the processes and procedures by which recommended credit is ratified and communicated to the student.
- Staff awareness of monitoring and evaluation that operate within their institution.

At the institutional level (macro quality), the key issue would seem to be that of evolving a policy that enables the micro quality to be realised. Within the policy and organisational aspects of macro quality is the administrative infrastructure, often so central to the development and maintenance of good practice. On the whole, the macro quality should, therefore, account for the following:

- the design and appropriateness of APL publicity material
- the ability to offer broad counselling and guidance services to intending students
- availability of facilities to maintain statistical data on applicants and their destinations
- provision of choices and clear separation, where appropriate, of APL from APEL for purposes of processing claims (see Figure 4)
- the co-ordination of APL activities from the different schools or faculties into a coherent quality assured APL service as shown in Figure 5.

The quality assurance issues represented in Figures 3–6 should not be seen as isolated from each other. They are meant to be complementary and simply represent different aspects of the quality assurance issues central to good practice. The nature of their complementarity is such that micro quality could not truly exist without macro quality and vice versa.

The monitoring and evaluation of APL provision, although normally co-ordinated centrally, can be carried out by programme teams or by administrative staff. Regardless of who actually carries out periodic evaluation of the APL service on offer, the key point is having a standard format. The standard format (see Figure 6) has the following advantages:

- It can be sent at any time to individuals or cohorts.
- It ensures the same evaluative information is sought over an agreed period of time.
- It facilitates comparison of perceptions of quality by different people.
- It facilitates the identification of strengths and weaknesses of the service.
- It enables positive trends and good practice to be identified and disseminated as appropriate.

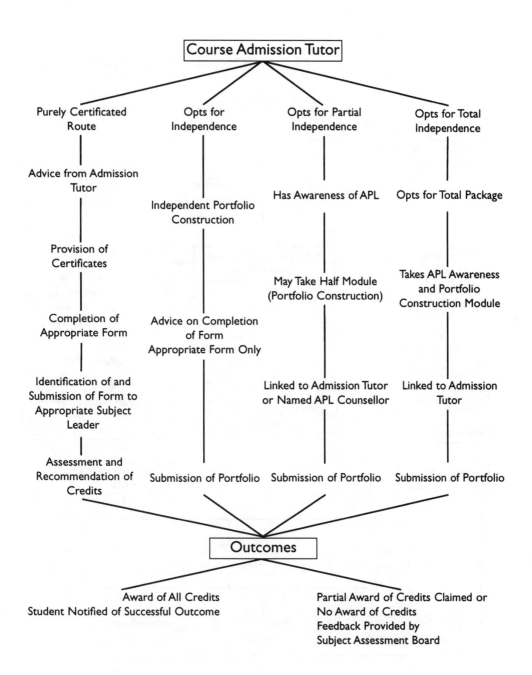

Figure 4 *Possible pathways for APL students*

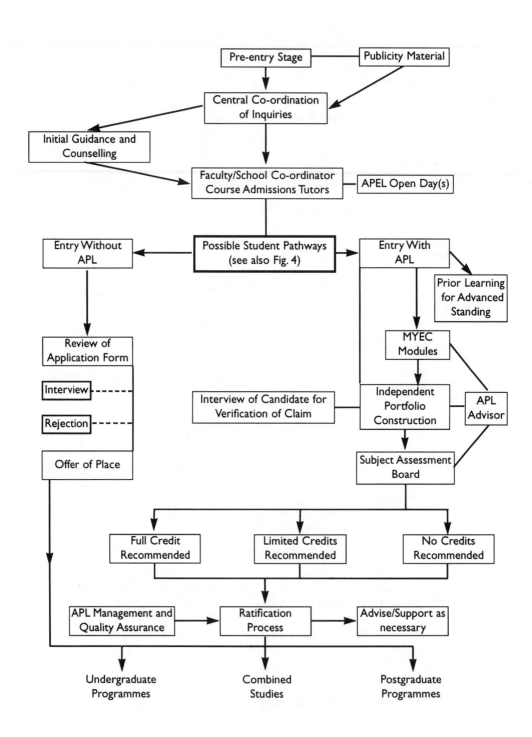

Figure 5 *Macro and micro APL processes*

In keeping with the quality assurance mechanism within the institution's APL regulatory framework, this evaluation form will be used to gather structured feedback from those involved in APL. For purposes of this evaluation APL and APEL will be synonymous. Please answer the following questions using the key provided.

Key to answers

1 = strongly agree with statement
2 = agree with statement
3 = not sure (either agree or disagree with statement)
4 = disagree with statement
5 = strongly disagree with statement

1.	The publicity material was clear and readily available.	1	2	3	4	5
2.	My APL inquiry at the university was handled in a helpful way.	1	2	3	4	5
3.	The APL process was explained to me.	1	2	3	4	5
4.	I was advised on the option of taking the MYEC modules to assist me with portfolio construction.	1	2	3	4	5
5.	I was made aware of the demands of APL including the need to provide appropriate evidence to support my claim.	1	2	3	4	5
6.	I was made aware of specific programme outcomes and how I could match these with my prior learning.	1	2	3	4	5
7.	The APL Advisor gave me support and guidance as appropriate.	1	2	3	4	5
8.	The APL process has enhanced my ability to reflect on my prior learning.	1	2	3	4	5
9.	I was made aware of the number of credits I could claim and the academic level appropriate to my claim.	1	2	3	4	5
10.	The staff kept me informed at each stage of the APL process and of the feedback process.	1	2	3	4	5
11.	I would recommend APL to other students who may have creditable prior learning.	1	2	3	4	5
12.	The cost of undergoing APL is reasonable considering the support I had and the process involved.	1	2	3	4	5

Please add any other recommendations or comments:

....
....
....
....
....
....
....

Figure 6 *APL evaluation form*

Thank you very much for the feedback.
You may put your name and programme if you wish.

Name ....

Programme or module ....

Year or stage ....

Please send your completed form to:

(Give address of coordinating office.)

Figure 6 *(contd.)*

As can be seen in Figure 6, the evaluation form addresses the micro as well as the macro issues. To this end it is important that all evaluations are co-ordinated centrally. The central co-ordination or monitoring is not there because of mistrust or fear of misuse of APL, it is there because it is an institutional provision with institutional ramifications for policy, finance and resources (see also Chapter 5, Organisational Context of APL). The quality of APL assessments undertaken by subject teams is subject to peer scrutiny through appropriate assessment boards/panels. Such panels (see Chapter 8) are useful in ensuring that procedures and processes all add up to the quality specifications expected by the institution and other agencies. It is further suggested that at both the micro and macro levels, it will be imperative to ensure or test out how academic and administrative standards are being realised at all levels of the service. The standards, as suggested by Whitaker (1989) are as follows.

Academic standards

* credit should be awarded only for learning and not for experience
* college credits should be awarded only for college-level learning
* credit should be awarded only for learning that has a balance, appropriate to the subject, between theory and practical application
* the determination of competence levels and of credit awards must be made by appropriate subject matter and academic experts
* credit should be appropriate to the academic context to which it is accepted.

Administrative standards

* credit awards and their transcript entries should be monitored to avoid giving credit twice for the same learning (double counting)
* policies and procedures applied to the assessment, including provision for appeal, should be fully disclosed and prominently available
* fees charged should be based on the services performed in the process and not on the amounts of credits awarded
* all personnel involved in the assessment of learning should receive adequate training for the functions they perform and there should be provision for their continued professional development
* assessment programmes should be regularly monitored, reviewed, evaluated and revised as needed, to reflect changes in the needs being served and the state of the assessment art.

It may be argued that the academic standards relate to micro quality issues, while the administrative standards relate to the macro quality issues. Obviously the distinction is not watertight. For instance, the fifth administrative standard can be carried out by academic staff with individual candidates or groups of APL candidates. The monitoring can also be carried out by administrative staff who may send questionnaires to candidates at strategic points within their study or after the students finish. All this information may be used centrally to improve or indeed maintain quality and standards. Part of good practice is to ensure institutions guard against possible misconceptions about APL. Misconceptions often lead to malpractice. Chapter 1 stated ten examples of malpractice (Nyatanga and Fox 1992) that were probably based on a number of misconceptions. The nature of some of these misconceptions will be discussed here. Some of the misconceptions seem to directly violate principles of good practice as well as the academic and administrative standards.

EIGHT APL MALPRACTICES

1. Granting credits for 'time served' or just experience: A few people found it difficult to separate experience from learning. Some people seemed unaware that experience and learning were two separate issues and that credit was only to be given for the actual learning as stated in Principle 2. (see Chapter 2)

2. Basing Assessment Fees on the number of credits awarded: APL is offered as a service to students in order to maximise individual potential for learning. It also recognises equal opportunity of access. As such, fees should relate to the service regardless of the number of credits. Like most programmes or modules the fees should be standard and declared in advance in order for students to assess whether or not they can afford it. In being charged fees per credit, students are unlikely to know the cost until their portfolio has actually been submitted and assessed. The dilemma this creates is that ability to pay and indeed withholding information on credits after a lot of effort has gone into producing a portfolio. This practice goes against administrative standard number 3.

3. Failing to separate the role of APL Advisor from that of Assessor: It is good practice to separate the two roles as this maximises objectivity. It is acknowledged there are institutions who would argue against this, perhaps on the basis that supervisors of independent studies, for instance, are advisors who often also assess the final piece of work. Perhaps good practice principle number 6 adequately takes into account the fact that advisors may not always be subject specialists. Indeed it is desirable that they are subject specialists but it is not imperative. To this end, and as reassurance of objective judgement, an advisor must not be involved in the direct assessment of the final portfolio.

4. Promising an APL service without regard for resources, staff development and expertise in the area: This misconception may simply be due to the fact that APL is sometimes perceived as common sense. This misconception therefore assumes no need for a co-ordinated service and quality assurance. According to administrative standard number 9 all personnel involved in APL should receive appropriate training. This also implies that the whole service should be authentic and quality assured.

5. Having no method of checking inconsistencies and APL malpractice: Offering unco-ordinated and inauthentic service. This point relates very closely to both the academic and administrative standards. This is an important issue central to the provision of an equitable and fair service to the users. It therefore follows that if APL is part of an insti-tutional commitment, it should have the same quality assurance measures as other pro-visions.

6. Failing to publicly declare in advance the rules, regulations and criteria used for APL assessment: If students are expected to produce portfolios in order to gain credits, then they must be given clear criteria. In the UK the criteria may include, inter alia, the learning outcomes to be satisfied, the APL principles and the time frame in which the APL process will take place. Both staff and students need to know this in advance.

7. Failing to provide a justified transcription of APL outcomes including sufficiency of evidence as part of quality assurance: Feedback to students and the issuing of tran-scripts (as appropriate) is an important part of the APL service. Feedback on the out-come of the portfolio assessment should normally be part of the standard APL service. Transcripts, on the other hand, can be issued on request. The institution, however, should have an agreed fee for the issue of a transcript to an individual.

8. Failing to check the authenticity of an APL claim: In a minority of cases students seemed to be promised admission or credits before the portfolio was even submitted for assessment. Perhaps this represents the intuitive knowledge some admission tutors claim they still use to determine the student's potential to benefit from a programme of study. APL, however is not about intuitive judgement of suitability, it is about objective and tangible evidence about learning. The checking of APL claims is thus seen through good practice principle 4 and administrative standard 6 as an important part of a qual-ity service.

GOOD PRACTICE SUMMARY

At the start of this chapter, it was suggested that quality may be defined as 'the degree of confidence that students and partner agencies have in relation to programme and institu-tional APL practices'. It was further suggested that authentic quality assurance systems will involve wider participation by significant others and that, in addition, they will be underpinned by effective communication in pursuit of shared aims and standards of prac-tice. The institution itself has to have a clear policy and commitment to staff development as part of control and enhancement of its quality assurance.

In summary, good practice in quality assurance requires that the institution has a clear quality assurance policy. Such policy should be supported by the clear regulatory frame-work within which APL operates. It should have regard for the principles of good practice, the micro and macro quality issues and administrative and academic standards. As a sum-mary, a good practice checklist will be presented under two subheadings, namely Macro (Administrative) Quality and Micro (Academic) Quality.

Macro (Administrative) quality

- The institution should have a clear APL policy which is translated into operational structures as shown in Figures 3-6.
- Have a marketing and publicity strategy.
- Ensure appropriate staff development at macro as well as micro quality level.
- Ensure there is in place an APL committee or board that oversees APL activities on behalf of the institution.
- Ensure proper co-ordination between the centre and the schools or faculties.
- Ensure communication channels for staff and students are clearly defined and well publicised.
- Ensure students understand their responsibilities within the APL process (see good practice principles).
- The administrative officer or office should have the following forms or their equivalent: (1) APL application form that combines certificated and non-certificated learning; (2) APCL form specifically for certificated learning and APEL form specifically for non-certificated learning.
- Administration office should also have (see Figure 6) an APL evaluation form and an APL monitoring log (see Appendix 2).
- Ensure programme annual reports include an evaluative section on APL experiences together with an appropriate action plan for the future (usually the following academic year).

Micro (Academic) quality

- Ensure programmes or modules have clear learning outcomes or competencies both staff and students can base their APL assessments on.
- Ensure programme leaders and admission tutors are conversant with APL principles and their application to assessment.
- Within the institution each school or faculty should have an APL co-ordinator to enhance subject-specific debate and feedback.
- Subject teams should have a nucleus of people capable of either advising on or assessing APL claims.
- Give appropriate support and feedback to students.
- Identify strengths and weaknesses of the APL provision through (a) self-evaluation (critical peer review); (b) institutional audit of artefacts (c) students' feedback; (d) external views and external examiner feedback. External views may include professional bodies, industry and commerce and funding bodies.
- Disseminate good practice in the accreditation of prior learning.

Chapter 5

Organisational Context of APL

INTRODUCTION

The introduction of APL will inevitably raise a number of issues which have a bearing upon the organisation as a whole. It will therefore require consideration from a management perspective in order to ensure effective planning and operation. The focus of this chapter therefore is to explore the key organisational decisions and strategies that will be required in order to fully establish APL policies and procedures within the organisation.

ORGANISATIONAL RATIONALE

The introduction of APL, at least in some organisations, has in the past arisen not from a carefully considered and implemented strategic plan generated against clear organisational goals or missions, but rather initiated as a result of a small-scale project or from a given individual's enthusiasm (Fox *et al.* 1992). More recently, however, and as stated in previous chapters (see Chapters 1 and 4), APL has been perceived as having strategic importance and indeed relevance to corporate goals. In consequence, it has increasingly been regarded as an issue for attention by strategic management. The reasons for recognising APL are numerous, and include drives or policy initiatives external to the education organisation itself (see also Chapter 6). While it is possible to explore only a few of these in this chapter, the central notion is that the organisation's strategic introduction of APL is but one vital approach to being both responsive and proactive to changing environments and markets within a competitive world. APL might therefore, at the extreme, be perceived as being a helpful strategy for organisational survival and development.

The organisational drives to strategically implement APL might be seen as including:

1. Drive of equal opportunity

A recognition that educational organisations have a role to play in enhancing equal opportunity and access to population groups that traditionally have lower uptake opportunities. This might include: individuals with a disability, people who perhaps due to redundancy/unemployment seek a retraining facility, women returning from a domestic role to employment, minority ethnic groups or individuals who due to prevailing social or financial circumstances were unable to follow career pathways.

2. Drive of consumerism

Consumer or customer responsiveness has become a favoured organisational motto of the early 1990s. This is true for many public education services. Indeed Field (1993) has suggested that one of the hallmarks of a successful college is its ability to know and respond to its customer needs. The significance given to educational organisations becoming responsive to consumer needs has been further reinforced within the Further and Higher Education Act of 1992. The Act, while wide-ranging in the issues it dealt with, did include an acknowledgement that in order to provide flexible quality-based education in a competitive environment, colleges would need to develop new approaches to teaching and learning in accord with identified need. A further and important indicator of the significance given to a consumer-orientated education is that of the Charter for Higher Education (1993).

Hence APL may be viewed by the organisation as one tool by which it exhibits its willingness to flexibly respond to individual or consumer needs.

3. Economic drive

Economic advantage is a natural and central concern for any organisation, with educational organisations being no exception. APL can readily be viewed as a mechanism that may contribute to such economic stability. For, while having many cost implications in itself, APL does have the potential to generate income, particularly through increasing the part-time student numbers. The financial significance of part-time recruitment is considerable in the light of restricted full-time student growth. Additionally, the provision of an APL facility can enhance a college's attractiveness to local employers seeking either an individual employee or group contract basis with continuing educational opportunities. Probably, as such an employer (while being committed to such employee development, perhaps due to investment in people policy) wishes to achieve this in the most cost-effective way perhaps, including academic recognition of work-based learning.

A further strategy used by many colleges to enhance financial robustness has been to widen the nature and range of courses it offers. Frequently this has meant embracing educational awarding bodies that already have a policy of APL. For example, the Business and Technology Educational Council (BTEC) and the English National Board for Nurses, Midwives and Health Visitors (ENB) have such a policy.

4. Quality assurance drive

Another important drive to embed APL within a college's central and strategic mechanisms, rather than to leave it as an individual initiative, has been the ever-increasing attention to the refinement of quality assurance and audit systems pertaining to all aspects of a college's activity. There is also a growing trend to try to attach financial gain to demonstrable quality standards and achievements. Thus quality assurance in this sense inevitably embraces APL in order to publicly attest to the underlying validity of the process.

5. A lifelong learning drive

The changing economic and working climate has fostered an increased recognition that, in tomorrow's world, few individuals will have a single or stable career pathway requiring exposure to education only at the career onset. Rather, educational opportunities will be required on a lifelong learning basis, in order to continually update transferable knowledge and skills as preparation for (potentially) a number of working roles. 1996 was designated the European year of lifelong learning and as such forced the recognition of the need to learn by both the old and the young. This, in itself, served to stimulate a more flexible approach to education. In particular, this has been via modular-based programmes of education, within which APL emerges as an important yet inevitable supporting mechanism, ensuring the learning is appropriate, avoids duplication and is economical for the individual and organisation.

Factors which drive organisational policies and activities of both an internal and external nature will inevitably influence the organisation's stated mission. This, in turn, should be both the starting point and rationale for any APL initiative.

APL AND THE ORGANISATIONAL MISSION

An organisational mission statement represents the predominant values, purpose and desires in terms of key activities and strategies. In order that it is meaningful, it has to be both accepted and operationalised by the people within the organisation and to embrace all key organisational functions. While the mission will require regular review and update, it should contain a perspective of both an immediate and future time frame in order to act as a 'guiding principle for planning and future development'. As Field (1993) suggests, the mission should embody the college's culture ethos. The principles of a mission statement, therefore, are that it should:

- be focused primarily upon satisfaction of the customer rather than achievement and product characteristics
- reflect the skills and attributes of the organisation
- realistically take account of environmental threats and opportunities
- be sufficiently specific so that it can influence organisational behaviour
- be attainable
- be flexible
- reflect external drives for change
- generate aims, objectives and developmental action plans.

It therefore follows, if an institution has within its mission statement any reference to enhancing equality of access, enhancement of its quality systems in support of admission or the desire to provide flexible and individually tailored programmes, then APL development is a clearly justifiable activity. As outlined in Chapter 4, APL is an integral part of CAMS and programmes that support it. It is a vehicle by which past uncertificated learning may also be systematically assessed and given appropriate credit. An illustrative example of the desired symbiotic relationship between a college's overall mission and its rationale for APL development is given below.

INSTITUTIONAL MISSION AND APL DEVELOPMENT

A plan for action

Identification of a rationale for APL development in accordance with the overall organisational mission will give rise to the need to develop an appropriate plan for action. The development of organisational action plans is a regular function of managers, the generic principles of which remain consistent when applied to APL. It is, therefore, to detailed consideration of such principles and their application that we now turn.

Obtaining approval for development

APL has an inevitable resource commitment even if its development is limited, perhaps limited to a course, rather than college wide. Nevertheless, it is likely that formal approval from the institution, and in some cases from professional bodies for the development of APL will be required. The strength of gaining formal approval is that it secures authority for action and decision-making for the designated programme.

- It reaffirms the organisation's commitment to providing appropriate resources
- It facilitates effective communication channels from the onset
- It secures agreement against targets and related dates and places the development in a quality and monitoring framework.

In a college context, each institution will have its own mechanisms for such formal approval and will have regard for the continuous improvement of quality. Generally, documents submitted for such approval will observe any institutionally agreed processes for the validation or approval of new programmes or frameworks and will address such central issues as:

- the context or justification of the development including relevance to the college mission and developmental plan
- the core activities or categories within the overall plan and sequence within which these must be accomplished
- assignment of responsibility to particular individuals or groups
- the allocation of resources required
- current levels of expertise available
- the level of organisational involvement, i.e. college wide, subject and course-specific
- review and monitoring of progress mechanisms and time periods.

The way in which such a proposal is presented for approval is often an important factor in enhancing its chance of acceptance. Again, key principles to be remembered whether the presentation is by document alone or supported by other evidence are:

- Persuasiveness, in that emphasis is given to the way in which APL meets the needs, concerns and goals of the organisation.
- Conciseness. Over-long explanations or excessive detail should be avoided, at this point only the important elements should be included.
- The presentation should be professionally organised, adopting an appropriate formality of style, and use selective data as necessary, for example, student profile/admission data pertaining to mature part-time students only.
- Personalisation, in that the message should be appropriate for and should engage the specific audience.

Specific questions likely to be of central concern at this approval stage of development will probably become the subject of more detailed action plans at a later stage. Initially, these may take the form of simple action schedules or, if the challenge of developments is more complex (for example, APL is to be introduced college wide), more accepted and comprehensive management/decision-making tools may be required. Among these are graphs, charts, programme evaluation and review technique (PERT) and critical pathways. Each of these can be vital organisational management aids to the organisation and help sequence work, facilitate communication and the review/monitoring of progress. Charts may be developed to reflect the entirety of the development and/or specific aspects such as the planning of staff development.

The generation of plans as a basis for both approval and action involves management decision-making against the items and strategies for inclusion within the plan. There are a number of decision-making models which may guide this process, together with a variety a decision-making tools which may prove helpful in establishing the priorities for consideration. Indeed, one of these is a further grid or chart system which seeks to overtly identify the range of possible alternative actions in supporting a given goal, the possible costs and savings, the potential staff effects together with effects on quality (Kerrigan 1991).

Managing change

The organisational development and introduction of APL must be viewed as representing a significant change process. Hence in the generation of the proposal and subsequent action plans, it is important that due recognition to change be given. There are numerous management of change theories and models that might be used as a point of reference; each gives due acknowledgement to the potential complexity of the management of change and its potential to generate organisational confusion and conflict.

Most straightforward and from a perspective of change (i.e. one which assumes change is accepted on the basis of its demonstrable merit and therefore does not emphasise strategies for addressing conflict), the model offered by Rogers and Shoemacher (1971) is helpful to consider. The model has three phases, each of which may be used for both global and more detailed development of action and decision-making plans, namely:

1. The invention or design of the change

This phase is perceived as including:

- submission of the proposal for approval
- identification of an APL co-ordinator
- drafting of documentation
- formation of relevant development committees/structure and groups
- clarification of all resource issues including, for example, an APL fee structure.

2. Diffusion (communication) of the information regarding the change

This phase potentially includes:

- staff awareness briefing
- inclusion of development detail and progress updates in newsletters
- reporting on progress to the appropriate committee
- structured staff development
- production of APL publicity material and inclusion within the college prospectus.

Tappen (1995) has suggested that key characteristics which will facilitate successful diffusion or communication include the identification of:

- the relative advantage of the new approach over old methods; such as, for example, the advantage of a formalised college-wide APL procedure over old single course exceptional entry practices
- its compatibility, in other words, its relationship to the strategic plan, current course portfolio, current admission procedures and perhaps, above all, clear reassurance pertaining to the transparent academic rigour and *equability* of the APL process
- its complexity, indicating the need to work through and share the various procedural, communication and administrative pathways involved in an APL submission and assessment, together with the development of appropriate supportive documentation
- the possibility of trying it out on a trial basis first
- the observation of the results, in other words, ways in which the process will be subjected to quality review and monitoring.

3. Consequences (adoption or rejection) of change

This phase includes issues such as:

- submission for approval/validation and adoption of the APL polices and procedures by way of definitive documentation to an appropriate group or body
- formal commencement and launch
- monitoring and quality assurance measures at onset of APL strategies and thereafter including the appointment of an external verifier including the possibility of a phased introduction.

Aspects of Change Requiring Particular Attention and Consideration

Within the overall strategy for the development and introduction of an organisational APL strategy there are four key aspects that are worthy of particular consideration and indeed exploration within this chapter, namely:

- harmonisation and relationship to other administrative pathways
- development of a marketing strategy
- development of a resource plan (including staff development)
- identification of an appropriate charging policy.

HARMONISATION AND RELATIONSHIP TO OTHER ADMINISTRATIVE PATHWAYS

The College will undoubtedly already have in place well 'tested and tried' administrative pathways, probably involving the College Registry and Faculty/School Offices. The pathways may be viewed as relating primarily to key functions such as:

- receipt and processing of a student's application
- maintenance of a student database
- systems to allow communication with both prospective and current students

- pathways to handle assessment documentation ensuring these are logged, forwarded to staff and external examiners and compiled for the consideration of appropriate committees and examination boards with the ultimate recording of results with the database
- internal pathways of communication with academic staff and registry to facilitate interview schedules and induction programmes and between registry and the finance department to ensure appropriate collection of fees.

Elements of these key administrative pathways will be overtly visible to staff and students alike through the publication of procedural guidelines and related documents. Although inevitable, the communication of such pathways will be of a different nature in terms of the staff and students, in other words, tailored to each of their needs.

It is important, therefore, when developing an APL policy and mechanism to ensure that due consideration is given to such existing pathways. As far as possible these may be utilised in support of the needs of the APL candidate. Utilisation of existing pathways will be preferable to the creation of new separate ones for APL, not only in terms of resource efficiency but also in terms of the avoidance of potential confusion and the facilitation of APL acceptance by the organisation and quality assurance. A core principle in the development and harmonisation of such administrative systems in support of APL is the identification of key points of authority and responsibility (see also Chapter 4). Such identification will serve to strongly influence the nature and forms of the administrative pathways developed. For example, is the responsibility of administratively receiving and processing the APL application to be vested with each Faculty/School Office or centrally? In what way does this reflect the responsibility vested for receipt and processing of more 'standard' applications of both a full-time and part-time student? Are there different administrative pathways for the applicant if undergraduate or postgraduate?

The pathways, while inevitably complex in reality, nevertheless require detailed identification in the form of regulations, guidance notes to both staff and prospective students and finally must be capable of being reduced from complexity to a more simple form in which diagrammatic or tabular communication flows may be created as a ready guide.

It is beyond the scope of this chapter to outline in full the mentioned regulations and guidance notes for staff and student. Accordingly, illustrative examples only are provided in terms of one small yet vital aspect of the administrative pathways in support of APL, namely the submission of a claim. Harmonisation will also need identification and formal approval in terms of the role of advisor, assessor and external verifier with these needing to be overtly related to the prescribed roles of, for example, external examiner. Similarly, the membership and terms of reference for relevant committee structures will need to be determined and approved, together with the identification of their relationship to other college committee structures and boards, for example, to any Academic Standard Committee and Academic Board.

A final, but perhaps all-important, area of administrative harmonisation will be that of the monitoring and quality assurance mechanisms. In part, these have already been alluded to in terms of the role of the external verifier and approval of the appropriate committee structure. However, over and above these quality 'pathways' will be the quality assurance mechanism which relates to the routine collection and monitoring of data as indicators, with this often being a central administrative function. Challis (1993) in discussion of this issue suggests that the generation of quality indicators for APL (and including related indicators of efficiency) might include consideration of the following:

- actual student enrolment as a ratio against target enrolment
- students completing the course as a ratio against student enrolment
- successful students as a ratio against students enrolled
- students' progress as a ratio against students completing
- the number of initial enquiries
- the number of learners following the APEL route
- the number of qualifications/units awarded through APEL
- other positive outcomes, e.g. work gained
- drop-out rules
- value-added factors, i.e. difference between leavers and completers
- the cost of key activities such as initial guidance, portfolio preparation support and assessment.

DEVELOPMENT OF A MARKETING STRATEGY

Marketing is one of the basic elements of an organisational development plan for APL. Marketing should at the onset influence the nature and form of an organisation's product (in this case the product being an APL mechanism), as well as influencing the associated cost structure, together with the matter of when the main APL activities should occur within the academic year. Marketing, therefore, is rather more than the production and distribution of publicity material. The multi-factorial nature of marketing can be illustrated by reference to Frain (1981) who identifies four key aspects of marketing, namely,

- marketing research
- marketing communications
- physical distribution
- personal selling.

This is a helpful framework for consideration of the key organisational issues pertaining to the marketing of APL.

Marketing research

The function of market research is primarily to determine the nature and level of demand likely to occur for APL, thus it helps to illuminate the key characteristics of the segment of the whole population that the college might serve who would value and seek APL opportunities.

Frain (1981) has suggested that key questions addressed by market research include:

1. Who are the actual and potential users of our product or service?
2. Where do they buy it?
3. When do they buy it?
4. Are they satisfied with it?
5. If not, can we improve it to their satisfaction?
6. What new products or service might they require?
7. How can we inform them about our product or service, i.e. what newspapers, magazines

or professional journals do they read?
8. What motives can we discern in the buying of our product or service?
9. What is the size of the total market for our product or service?
10. What is our share of the market?.

These questions are commonly answered by the undertaking of a community profile to explore such issues as age, gender, employment and ethnic mix patterns. Thus providing an initial insight into the characteristics of likely students, further enquiry might also help to give some indication as to the factors which might influence a student's selection of one college as opposed to another, or indeed key factors that might influence a student progressing an initial enquiry to that of a formal application.

This information can give vital direction to both marketing and recruitment strategies and indeed may also serve to influence staff training, for example the way in which initial telephone enquiries are answered or the fee structure that might realistically be acceptable given the local economic trends.

Marketing communications

The development of a good service or product alone is insufficient; it is vital that its existence is made known to the potential buyer or student. This is essentially the purpose of marketing communications which typically uses a range of approaches. Field (1993) has suggested these may be classified as:

- advertising, which consists of the purchase of space in newspapers, television, cinema, local radio or outdoor space/locations. Frequently, a local 'freepost' mail may be used to encourage segments of the population
- sales promotion, this being complementary to advertising and consisting of exhibitions, or displays, perhaps in local stores, libraries, theatres, etc.
- publicity, often of a 'free' nature, by means of local editorials, radio or television programmes.

A marketing communication perhaps worthy of particular consideration is that of the 'Open Day' which may be either dedicated to APL or of a more general nature in which there is an opportunity to explore a range of courses, etc. provided by a college and within which specific space is given for individuals to learn about the APL opportunities if wished. The staging of an open event embraces each of the three categories offered by Field above. Further, it serves to demonstrate the interdependent nature of the marketing department and the total educational organisation. An open event involves the attendance of academic staff as advisors, clerical/administrative staff to allow registration and payment of fees, portering and catering staff to provide refreshments for those attending and a suitable room layout and porting and securing staff. Additionally, of course, it involves the generation via the marketing officer/department of specific advertising to announce the event, displays at the venue for the open event and general publicity to ensure maximum awareness of the event. Equally, the marketing activity of an open event may involve the follow-up of individuals who attended (both those who later applied for admission and those who did not) as a means of evaluating the event and related publicity in order to learn lessons for the future and thereby influence the marketing strategy thereafter.

Physical distribution

Frain (1981) discusses the notion of physical distribution against the economic principle of utility, namely, the ability of the product to satisfy a demand. He suggests that such utility can be seen as having a number of attributes, i.e.:

a) *A utility of form* in that the product must be in the form required. Thus the way in which APL portfolio construction advice/counselling is given may be shared by knowledge of the consumers' preferences. For example, should it be through group activities, distance/open learning, telephone tutorials or help lines or individual-based college attendance.

b) *A utility of place,* i.e. available at a location convenient to the user. This issue, therefore, raises questions about the way in which the market research can inform the location of supportive APL activities, APL counselling and the provision of related portfolio modules. Should this be on the main college campus or located on a number of outreach sites within the community?

c) *A utility of time,* i.e. available when it is required, again influencing the pattern of provision for APL guidance and counselling opportunities. Should those be in the form of evening, morning or whole day/weekend activities?

Decisions about each of the above are an important marketing issue influencing the possible 'take-up' of the APL mechanism once developed.

Personal selling

Marketing communication may be through strategies designed to reach the mass audience, however, it is important to recognise that another important element in the marketing process is that of personal contact. Such contact is often a powerful selling vehicle. As with mass communication, the exchange is intended to provide information about the nature of the product, i.e. APL. In this context, it is important to recognise that a wide number of individuals within the organisation may be undertaking 'personal selling' and this may not be restricted to those individuals who formally have this as part of their official role. It is equally possible that a potential APL student's first port of contact may be the college receptionist or gardener as well as a member of the academic staff, as initial contact may be of the informal as well as of a more purposeful nature. This, therefore, raises the question as to how all staff may be given a general awareness, at least sufficient that they are able to redirect an initial enquiry to an appropriate point in the organisation for more detailed information. This reaffirms the need for general communication about the development via college newsletters or staffroom displays produced perhaps via the marketing department, as well as more focused and formal staff development activities.

The questions posed by Challis (1993) offer a helpful view of this latter point:

1. Do we have a target audience identified and a proposed means of reaching them?
2. Do we have supporting publicity?
   a) on the concept of APEL?
   b) on APEL within selected programmes?
3. Does the whole staff know about APEL and where it is on offer?
4. Do we have a standard first enquiry form so that we can monitor requests for APEL?
5. Do the reception staff know how and to whom to refer potential APEL enquiries?

Therefore, and to summarise, marketing must be seen as a significant element in the organisational considerations in support of APL in order that the development and final form of the APL procedures offered are both relevant to the potential students' needs and that consumers are aware of the existence of APL as an opportunity designed specifically to meet their needs.

DEVELOPMENT OF A RESOURCE PLAN

Many aspects of APL demand a resource commitment in terms of actual financial allocation, dedication of staff time (both academic and support staff) and use of college premises/equipment. Such a resource commitment is evident in the initial development of the APL mechanism, its marketing, its operation in terms of initial advice, guidance and assessment and finally its monitoring and evaluation with quality assurance. Nevertheless, Challis (1993) suggests that once established APL 'can operate at least as cost effectively as the traditional course led pattern' (p. 134). This view was based upon the financial analysis of a pilot scheme with a college in Sheffield. To ensure such equitable cost, Challis reaffirms the necessity for organisations to plan the systematic development and operation of APL. This could be on a selected or college wide basis. She suggests that among the strategies which might be used to minimise cost are:

* time tabling tutors into workshops where teaching and assessment takes place
* extending the college year so that more consistent and frequent use is made of staff and accommodation
* using support staff for some of the initial screening of learners
* switching money between budget leads in order to pump-prime the system.

Certainly, the initial development of APL is acknowledged to be resource-intensive, which serves to reaffirm the advantage of committing development at a strategic level against the mission of the college at the onset. Again, Challis (1993) has suggested a number of organisational options by which resources for APL might be identified. These include the top slicing of a development budget, the establishment of a separate central APL dedicated budget and the allocation of proportional APL funds to school/faculties.

In a limited number of instances, developmental partners might be found to share the burden of costs and other external funds, successfully bid for (Fox *et al.* 1992).

Clearly, a significant factor in the set up costs associated with APL is that of staff development, with this being an issue that must be accounted for within the overall resource plan. Staff development as justified earlier within this chapter must embrace:

* all staff in terms of general awareness raising
* clerical/support staff, potentially those who might be the first point of contact in a student enquiry, who have to process the APL claim and finally those who help generate the supporting database
* academic staff in the capacity of both advisor and assessor. Recently, many colleges have elected to undertake this via training and development lead
* institutional induction for the appointed external examiner
* those staff members who are part of any specific APL committee/reporting structure.

The commitment of resources to such staff development will reward the organisation in facilitation of: a reduced resistance and acceptance of change that accompanies the introduction of APL, an increased customer satisfaction, entrance quality and will be cost-effective in terms of the reduction of error or time wasted due to the lack of clarity. In many organisations, the commitment of resources in this way to staff development will be fully in accordance with existing resource allocation, particularly where there is already a commitment to be an organisation which invests in its staff.

Clearly, there are a number of strategies which might be used to facilitate such staff development, including videos, distance learning packs, role play, simulation activities and group discussion.

Additionally, there will be other staff development programmes which have a complementary development role to APL, for example, training staff in counselling skills.

Clearly, while such staff development is of primary importance at the onset of an APL strategy, it is also important to ensure that a smaller but continuing resource commitment is not simply required to accommodate increased uptake and growth of APL and staff turnover, but also to allow staff refreshment and update as a means of ensuring ongoing quality relevance and development of the APL procedures.

CHARGING POLICY

The establishment of a charging policy is demonstrably a significant issue to the organisation not only in terms of influencing the attractiveness of the APL mechanism to the customer but also serving to recoup at least in part, some of the moneys dedicated by the organisation to the development and operation of APL.

Within recent years, a number of charging policies have been in operation. Some have adapted the principle of a loss leader in the hope it will attract later full fee customers, others have operated on a full cost recover basis at the onset and thereafter seeking a middle road, providing some advice free initially and a sliding scale of fees thereafter dependent upon the level of service/support. A number of organisations, in order to seek harmonisation of APL charging with that of other courses offered by the organisation, have provided accredited modules on a normal module fee basis in support of portfolio construction advice. A further strategy adopted has been levying the fee charges against the sum of moneys saved by the student in achieving credit against a standard course, while some colleges have charged by classification of the student. Whatever the policy adopted, there remain some guiding principles, namely:

- the cost to the prospective student must be clearly identified at the onset
- the mechanisms for collection must be simple and cost-effective
- the fee must be such that it is at a level which makes it worthwhile to collect, i.e. more than the cost of administrative recovery
- the fee must be set at a level that makes it attractive to the customer yet perceived as being equitable against other charging policies
- the cost must be demonstrable 'value for money' against the source provided
- the fee must be clearly competitive in comparison with the APL charging policy of other institutions.

Challis (1993) has again offered some helpful questions that might be asked in determining the fee – should charging be on the basis of:

a) hourly vocational rates estimated and actual time taken?
b) hourly non-vocational rates estimated and actual time taken?
c) a block charge per phase of the APL process (e.g. initial guidance, profiling, portfolio preparation support, assessment)?
d) ability to pay?
e) outcome as compared with the cost of achieving the same ends through a taught course? (module or unit equivalent fee)
f) Should there be a group purchase discount?

Finally, it is perhaps worthwhile for an organisation to remember the old adage that not money but quality is often the final determinant when establishing its charging policy.

GOOD PRACTICE SUMMARY

This chapter has considered the complex and wide-ranging issues that the development and introduction of an APL mechanism poses to an organisation. In summary, it has been shown that each stage of the APL process has organisational implications (see Figures 3 and 4). A number of 'checklists' have been produced by which an organisation may appraise its adequacy of planning for and operating of the APL process. Additionally, the authors suggested at the beginning of this chapter that organisations may find it advantageous to develop their action checklists and plans pertaining to both the total development of an APL strategy and management elements within it.

There are a number of principles of good practice that can be stated as follows:

- Recognise the value of strategically managed development.
- Recognise the introduction of APL as requiring the management of change.
- Attempt as far as possible to harmonise APL regulations, policies, procedures and related committee structures with others within the institution.
- Identify appropriate resources in support of initial APL development and thereafter.
- Seek to establish APL as a recognised function valued by all rather than a 'Cinderella Activity'.
- Ensure APL information is clearly identified and tailored to meet student and staff needs and is freely available and current.
- APL should be managed organisationally in such a way that it can be demonstrably economic, quality-based, supportive to the college strategic aims, enhance equality and opportunity and above all, be embedded within the college's culture and daily operations.

Chapter 6

APL: An Evolving Agenda

INTRODUCTION

The two main issues to be considered in this chapter are related to the forces or drives behind the APL initiatives and some of the research influencing current debate on APL. The spirit of the various types of credit accumulation and transfer schemes (CATS) is shared by the UK and a number of European institutions. The spirit is to do with facilitating systematic student mobility through recognition of learning acquired from participating institutions. In the UK, the harbinger of the CATS system can be traced back to 1970 when The Open University started offering credit-based programmes and seeking agreement with other UK institutions for mutual recognition of those credits. Two further aspects by which CATS was to be fully realised were the modularisation of programmes with their related learning outcomes and the assessment of prior learning (APL). In this sense APL is particularly important as it also seeks to acknowledge formal as well as informal learning that would not normally be covered by institutional CATS arrangements. Thus APL supports the CATS principles by additionally offering a mechanism and process by which individuals can seek assessment and accreditation of any relevant learning not already credited. The use of the phrase 'any relevant learning' is deliberate and has been used to denote a link not only with stated learning outcomes but also with valid and reliable assessment methods. To return to the theme of this chapter, the following section will explore some of the political and social forces or drives that have helped place APL on many institutions' agendas.

THE ROBBINS RECOMMENDATIONS

Educational developments between 1960 and the year 2000 represent radical changes in UK institutions. Of the major reports to be given credit for shaping the changes, Lord Robbins' report of 1963 is probably the most notable. Subsequent to the Robbins report other recommendations such as those of the three committees chaired by Sir Ron Dearing and other reports have added and refined issues raised in the Robbins report. Schuller (1995) cites the CVCP (1994) whose current social and political perception of education is that universities are now key players in their respective local economy. It is claimed CVCP go on to suggest that higher education is likely to be among the biggest employers accountable to local communities and covering a number of societal needs. Higher education should deliver services to citizens, as undergraduates, graduates and postgraduates or continuing education to local employers and beyond. Thus before looking at the implications of this perception or philosophy for APL, perhaps the question has to be 'how did this philosophy come on to the agenda'. The answer lies largely in the Robbins and Dearing reports.

The Robbins report 1963

Starting in the early 1960s, the Robbins report brought about immense educational changes. The report had the following impacts:

* It created an expansion of student numbers entering higher education.
* It set parameters and criteria for new universities.
* It transformed many colleges of advanced technology into polytechnics.
* The concept of polytechnics and The Open University were generated through the Robbins report.
* The Council for National Academic Awards (CNAA) was also established to co-ordinate quality and standards.
* The Department of Education and Science (DES) was created in order to assume responsibility from the treasury.
* There was a marked increase in overseas student fees.

It could be argued that the Robbins report created the current political philosophy of mass education. Indeed the impact of the Robbins report was not always pre-seen. It nevertheless started a wave of changes that are still being acted upon at present and beyond. It could be argued the changes suggested by the Robbins report were only tentative in the sense that the creation of The Open University and polytechnics had not been seen as a direct attempt to widen access to higher education. Instead the idea was to offer a different type of education and training not at the time accessible through traditional universities. Thus the advent of polytechnics brought with it the political drive towards applied skills. The applied skills were being introduced at a time when questions about the correlation between academic courses and the extent to which they prepared individuals for employment were being asked. The development in the late 1980s of the concept of enterprise skills and the funding of such research projects as 'what can graduates do' signal the importance of this political drive. The success achieved by both the OU and polytechnics may have directed attention to the differences and indeed similarities between traditional universities and these newer provisions. The eventual demise in 1992 of the binary line between traditional universities and polytechnics suggest there were more similarities than differences in both quality and standards.

In terms of CATS, modularisation and APL both the OU and polytechnics were already discussing the best ways of harmonising the arrangements (see Chapter 1). The removal of the binary line therefore meant further harmonisation of policies and philosophies on admissions to programmes, lifelong learning and accreditation of prior learning. The sceptic will probably see all this as no more than a move to mass education. To add to the anxieties of the sceptic there is also the drive to develop a framework of qualifications (see Figure 7) capable of linking academic and vocational qualifications. The qualifications framework is a sound outline conducive to the ideology of lifelong learning and accreditation of prior learning. It will be argued later that the whole concept of lifelong learning and in particular APL has been the acid test which seemingly still proves that elitist values continue to heavily influence mass education ideology.

THE QUALIFICATION FRAMEWORK

Attempts are being made to link academic qualifications with vocational or competency based qualifications. These have traditionally been separate entities that have made the students' life difficult as progression pathways have always been unclear if not non-existent. It is also fair to suggest that the qualification framework is a necessary drive seeking to bring colleges of further and higher education (mainly using NVQs & GNVQs) closer together with universities (mainly using academic levels & CATS). Recent evidence (*The Times Higher*, 23 August 1996) suggests that the harmonisation represented in Figure 7 may well be starting to work. According to this article, students with GNVQ are:

- Getting into top research universities
- Getting admission for further study in prestigious universities
- Gaining the same success rate when compared with students entering through the A-level route

The then Secretary of State for Education and Employment (Gillian Shephard) confirmed that vocational qualifications were gaining more acceptance from the wider academic community. It was also revealed that individuals taking top level vocational qualifications such as NVQ levels 4 & 5 or GNVQ levels 3 & 4 rather than degrees were more likely to get highly paid jobs than traditional graduates. While this last claim may be political propaganda, the key point is the acceptance and comparability of the qualifications framework.

Table 5 *Educational developments: summary of four decades*

Report/committee	Key developments	Possible mission
Robbins Report 1963	Polytechnics The Open University CNAA DES	Adult learners' academic needs Professional & vocational needs Monitor quality & standards Funding arrangements
1970 Open University initiates credit-based programmes	Credit transfer feasibility study (Toyne 1979) Widespread use of credits	Seek credit transfer agreement with other institutions Credit consortia established with the encouragement of the then CNAA
The Oakes committee 1977	Establishment of NAB in February 1982 Removal of local authorities in 1989 Demise of binary line in 1992	National Advisory Body (NAB) was to advise on local authority education Freedom to manage learning Freedom to learn
NVQ & GNVQ 1988 & 1991 respectively	NVQs cover competency levels 1-5 GNVQs cover both knowledge and skills levels 1-4 of vocational qualifications	NVQs address the competencies necessary for specific employment GNVQs attempt to bridge the gap between theoretical and practical issues
Sir Ron Dearing 1989	Creation of PCFC in 1989 Creation of PCFCE 1992 Demise of CNAA	Mainly funding across all institutions Funding for England Creation of HEQC based with Open University

The new institutions (the polytechnics and The Open University) were initially funded separately by DES. This also signalled that these institutions were a kind of project to be tested and evaluated before being accepted. They, however, were fulfilling an educational need and indeed a niche which traditional universities ignored altogether. The niche was to do with two categories of students, namely:

- Adults seeking a second chance to improve their education (would go to polytechnics)
- Adults seeking professional or vocational qualifications (Open University).

The Open University was linked more closely with fulfilling employment needs and the needs of employers. Against this background and indeed looking at complementary activities in modularisation, credit transfer and accreditation of prior learning, two key issues emerge. These are:

- The predominant political ideology is that of lifelong learning which encompasses notions of equal opportunity, accessibility and accreditation of prior learning including prior experiential learning The ideology is gaining momentum and support despite being created as an alternative to traditional academic pursuits of the pre-Robbins days. (see also Section 5).
- The political shift to mass education has created, in some quarters, a dialectic tension of educational beliefs and values. This dialectic tension is best exemplified in the area of APL. APL, in this sense, represents the widest opening of education doors to the masses. In the views of some people, such massification destroys the very essence and special nature of education. In some ways, the whole notion of credit accumulation and transfer is guilty of over-massification. On the positive side, there have always existed educational and curriculum philosophies that can be said to be compatible with APL initiative and drives (Nyatanga and Fox 1996).

From Chapter 1 it can be seen that the use and implementation of APL is relatively nascent. It therefore follows that APL-related research within the UK would be relatively new and on a small scale. However, within the 11 years that APL has existed in the UK, a number of significant areas have been investigated. For instance there has been research in such areas as:

- The consistency of APL assessment decisions (City & Guilds 1990)
- Good practice in the accreditation of prior learning (Nyatanga and Fox 1992)
- Investigation into the validity and reliability of assessment strategies for the accreditation of prior learning of nurses, midwives and health visitors (English National Board 1997)
- The problem of educational levels: conceptualising a framework for credit accumulation and transfer (Winter 1993)
- Choosing to change: extending access, choice and mobility in higher education (HEQC 1994).

KEY ISSUES EMANATING FROM THE VARIOUS RESEARCH PROJECTS

The consistency of APL assessment decisions project, probably one of the first projects within the National Vocational Qualification (NVQ) area, was carried out to test, among other objectives, the consistency of APL assessment decisions across chosen NVQ centres and to establish if APL was prone to any greater degree of unreliability than conventional assessments.

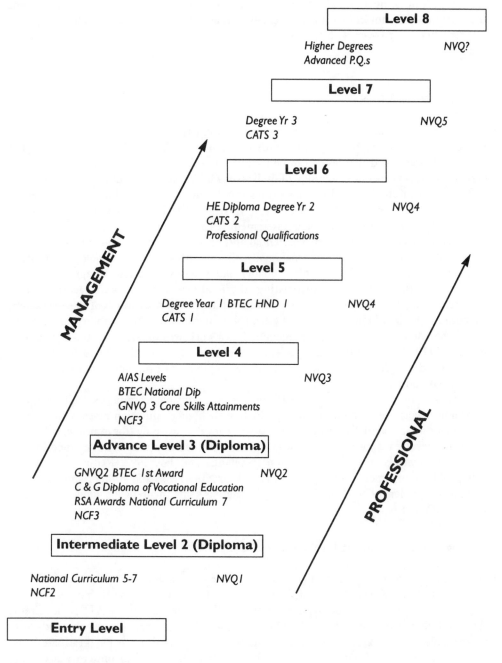

Figure 7 *Qualifications framework*

Although the study itself did not find tangible evidence to support 'the consistency of APL assessment decision' claim, it acknowledged that the credibility of APL would heavily depend on some scientific or systematic evidence of its reliability as an assessment tool. The project also signalled a challenge to conventional methods of assessment that they too may not be as reliable or consistent as first assumed. The challenge is even greater when interwoven with the issue of academic levels and their utility in higher education.

ACADEMIC LEVELS

Academic levels of learning are a common concept in British higher education assessment frameworks. So this chapter reports a study that considers the theoretical basis of levels of learning. It was noted that levels can be usefully conceptualised and described as generic (a national consensus understanding of each level which transcends subject areas) and thematic (an institute-, discipline- or profession-specific understanding of each level). Implications for the Accreditation of Prior Learning (APL), the Recognition of Prior Learning (RPL) and Prior Learning Assessment (PLA) are discussed.

Awarding academic credit for experiential and prior learning from outside institutes of higher education is practised internationally. Practitioners share terminology, standards and commitment to flexible learning, quality and progress (see also Chapter 1). Many experience other educators mistrusting these alternative forms of accreditation. Differences in practice of accreditation may be influenced by the context of the assessment framework within which practitioners work (Nyatanga 1993). The reliability and validity of assessment is limited by the assessment framework within which credit is awarded. Nyatanga (1993) argues that thus far sharing ideas and a commitment to research and theory-based progression has facilitated the development of prior and experiential learning accreditation.

Simosko (1988) and Lamdin (1992) discuss recognising learning as 'college level'. Academic levels are a common concept in British higher education assessment frameworks. But what is actually meant by an academic level of learning (for example, college or university level learning)? Previous research has identified that what is understood by academic levels needs further investigation (Nyatanga and Fox 1992, Redfern and James 1994). Novice to expert theories (Dreyfus and Dreyfus 1980) and student approaches to learning (Ramsden 1979, Biggs 1991) suggest there is some theoretical evidence for generic levels of learning.

Assessment of academic levels in the UK

It has already been suggested that academic levels are a common concept in British assessment frameworks. Some of these frequently used assessment frameworks for higher education are Credit Accumulation and Transfer Scheme (CATS) and Credit Accumulation Modular Scheme (CAMS). These schemes normally divide study into progressive levels 1, 2 and 3 at undergraduate level and level 'm' at postgraduate level. The Scottish Credit Accumulation and Transfer Scheme uses four undergraduate levels of learning. For these schemes to be relevant and for transfer (from programme to programme) to occur there should be a national understanding of each level of learning

(Otter 1991, Redfern and James 1994). However, at the present time there are diverse descriptions of levels of learning across institutes for nursing (Redfern and James 1994). It has not been established whether such diversity is relevant to other professions and disciplines. So, a study was undertaken to identify theoretically based working descriptions of levels of learning through the consensus opinion of health educators.

In the Scottish Credit Accumulation and Transfer Scheme (SCOTCATS) there are four undergraduate levels. At the University of East Anglia there are two undergraduate levels. There is some theoretical evidence for generic levels of learning:

1. novice to expert theories (Dreyfus and Dreyfus 1980)
2. student approaches to learning (Ramsden 1979, Biggs 1991).

The vital link between academic levels and APL

- The validity and reliability of APL and APEL relies on assessment frameworks, which are based on the concept of level of learning (Winter 1993).
- For national schemes like CATS and CAMS to be relevant and for transfer from institute to institute at the same level to be appropriate there should be a national understanding of each level of learning (Otter 1991, Redfern and James 1994). At the present time there are diverse descriptions of levels of learning across institutes for nursing (Redfern and James 1994).
- A national understanding of each level of learning is difficult to accomplish because descriptions of levels are often derived from:

    1. institutional mission statements (Allen 1988)
    2. quality control mechanisms (Hall 1993)
    3. a method of placing a course or module in a wider framework.

Therefore, a study to identify theoretically based working descriptions of levels of learning through the consensus opinion of health educators was undertaken.

Epistemological basis of academic levels

Generic descriptions of levels (academic and expert) can be gained. This is in agreement with Redfern and James' (1994) and Otter's (1991) view that there should be a national understanding of each level. This is compatible with Fenwick *et al.* (1992) who claim to have identified skills which transcend subject areas.

But:

- Knowledge and skills are learnt and embedded in context (Becher 1989, Mandl *et al.* 1991)
- There is no theoretical grounding for transferable skills (English 1992)
- Different disciplines or professions can have different characteristics at the same level (Fenwick *et al.* 1992).

Generic and thematic levels

These opinions and results indicate there may be two types of level descriptions: thematic and generic descriptions. Thematic descriptions of level would be an institute- and subject- or profession-specific description of the national understanding of each generic level.

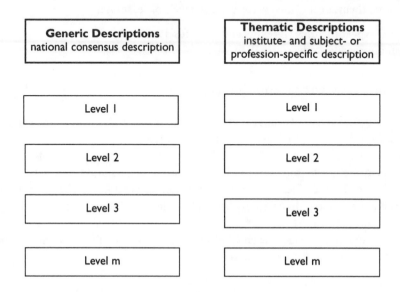

Figure 8 *Generic and thematic levels*

Examples of generic descriptions of academic levels

Level 1

- the learner exhibits little self-regulation or autonomy and is reliant on the teacher for direction and motivation
- the learner is unaware that his/her theoretical knowledge is partial and fragmented
- the learner can be biased or inaccurate in his/her description and selection of material
- in the few opportunities available the learner applies general principles and abstract criteria with difficulty
- the learner will occasionally question the content of material
- the learner believes that, for any given situation, knowledge is based on the most credible explanation which the learner awards factual status and assumes to be the truth
- the learner can only think of either logical possibilities or logical deductions for the same situation
- the format used by the learner to organise and connect concepts in his/her memory replicates the format of the original material
- when the learner encounters new material he/she often finds it hard to remember
- the learner's work is subjective.

Level 2

- the learner exhibits some self-regulation or autonomy and can be reliant on the teacher for direction and motivation
- the learner generally knows how and when to apply knowledge, but is not clear why he/she has done so
- the learner will make some errors in learning and problem solving
- the learner has a general understanding of concepts, theories and the relationships between them.
- the learner can criticise and evaluate although this is not always effective
- the learner has his/her own perception of information but cannot produce new knowledge
- the learner evaluates his/her learning, with restricted understanding
- the format used by the learner to organise and connect concepts in his/her memory partially replicates the format of the original material
- when the learner encounters new material he/she sometimes finds it hard to remember.

Level 3

- the learner is unbiased and accurate in his/her analysis, critique and selection of material
- the learner exhibits self-regulation or autonomy with some reliance on the teacher for direction and motivation
- the learner tries to apply general principles and abstract criteria to new situations
- the learner is aware of the existence and nature of concepts, theories and relationships between them, some of which pertain to his/her specialist area
- the learner knows how, why and when to apply knowledge
- the learner's work is objective
- the learner will solve problems with a very high success rate
- the learner can think of both logical possibilities and logical deductions for the same situation.

Level 4

- the learner exhibits self-regulation and autonomy and is in a position to disseminate knowledge
- the learner has their own personal perception of extensive theoretical knowledge and can produce new knowledge in a specialist area (synthesis and extrapolation)
- the learner will rarely have misconceptions while learning.

Issues that divide

There are several issues that seemingly continue to divide and indeed hinder the development of an absolutely agreed definition of generic academic levels. Some of the issues may be summarised as follows:

- Universities have different purposes and mission statements which greatly influence definitions of academic levels. Some of these purposes are not always apparent even to

staff implementing them
- Module learning outcomes incorporating:
    1) an institution's mission statement
    2) the culture of the dominant discipline
    3) views of dominant professional bodies.

Evidence from one of the HEQC (1997) projects suggests further dividing issues with regards to the notion of academic levels. In this particular project 'Assessment in higher education and the role of graduateness' which is one of the series of projects commonly known as the 'Graduate Standards Programme' the issue of academic levels is recognised and raises the following dividing perspectives:

- that inter-institutional differences continue to exist with respect to expected learning outcomes and the way these are recognised through assessed work
- that the same terminology such as shows critical evaluation, demonstrates synthesis, shows originality and so forth are used at various academic levels which makes comparisons difficult
- that much of the terminology used in higher education is also used in further education institutions to describe A level work or achievement
- that there may be confusion between marking criteria and definition of academic levels. Terminology as used above may reliably be used to compare attainment of students at a given level rather than determining whether or not they are at that given level. Thus students who pass or fail will be considered as having attempted assessments at a given level. A number of institutions have developed marking/grading descriptors that can be associated with degree classification (see Table 6)

Table 6 *Grading/marking descriptors*

Descriptor	Report grade	Degree class	Traditional %
Outstanding work, exceptionally high standard, excellent	A+		90+
Excellent work in most respects, insightful and original (very minor defects)	A	First	80–89
Very good work with a few minor defects	A-		70–79
Very good standard of work (with a few defects)	B+		67–69
Generally very good standard of work (but with some defects)	B	Upper Second	63–66
Good standard of work (but with some notable defects)	B-		60–62
Good and credible standard of work (but with a few notable defects)	C+		57–59
Generally good standard of work (but with a number of notable defects)	C	Lower Second	53–56
Generally good standard of work (but with a significant number of defects)	C-		50–52
Fair standard of work (but has a number of shortcomings)	D+		47–49
Satisfactory standard of work (but with a number of significant shortcomings)	D	Third	43–46
Acceptable minimum standard of work (with a significant number of major but acceptable shortcomings)	D-		40–42
Borderline Pass/Fail, generally unsatisfactory standard of work	P	N/A	35–39

It can be seen from Table 6 that grade descriptors can easily be confused with level descriptors presented earlier in this chapter. The grade descriptors are supposedly concerned with standard of work at a given level. As such the authors have witnessed these descriptors used for Business Technician Education Council (BTEC) programmes as well as university designed academic programmes. In one sense the overlap creates issues about the essence of the differences. This is not to say there are no differences at all, rather it is about being able to identify and quantify those differences in a way that enhances current understanding of academic levels.

GOOD PRACTICE SUMMARY

- Generic descriptors of academic levels should be pursued and expanded through the use of Delphi methodology. This approach will confirm the essential attributes of graduates and indeed postgraduate students.
- Thematic (discipline-specific) descriptors of academic levels should also be developed perhaps using signal detection theory and its related methodology. This will enable subject areas or disciplines to detect professional and academic attributes central to their area of concern. The detected attributes may then be used not only as APL portfolio assessment criteria but also as a basis for personal and professional development where this is appropriate.
- Grading/marking descriptors must be separate from academic level descriptors.
- As institutions seek to maximise the use of modular schemes and CATS they should also have regard for comparability of standards and quality assurance across institutions. Where professional bodies are involved greater consultation should lead to the development of acceptable threshold standards.
- Portfolio assessment like other assessments should strive to attain transparency of standards especially within the same or similar disciplines.
- Adequate resources especially administrative and academic staff development have to be at the forefront of any committed institution.

Part Two

Worked Examples of Two Portfolios

Introduction

As stated in Part One, this section of the book presents chosen portfolio examples that illustrate the link between the theoretical perspectives and practice.

Chapter 7 presents a portfolio developed against Management Charter Initiatives (MCI) and Chapter 8 presents a modular degree portfolio based on the discipline of horticultural studies. This particular portfolio represents the industrial placement element of the BSc Horticulture.

Each chapter contains a portfolio capable of illustrating two applied perspectives. The first perspective is that APL is operated against a variety of academic awards which may include competencies or skills and cognitive ability often expressed in learning outcomes. The second perspective is the illustration of the actual process that leads to award of credits. For each of the portfolios, the process will emphasise different perspectives.

For instance, in Chapter 7, the process emphasises the variety and range of evidence required for the MCI competencies. This also explains why Chapter 7 is comparatively much longer than the rest.

In Chapter 8 the process emphasises the quality control function that may constitute good practice for institutions committed to APL. Thus the chapters help illustrate issues about the nature of evidence, the role of the assessors and the institutional quality assurance mechanism (see also Chapter 4). The authors acknowledge that communication and administrative arrangements are an integral part of good practice. However, due to space, these have been addressed only in Part One (see Chapters 1 and 4). Notwithstanding this fact, it is hoped these worked examples will enhance the debate and appreciation of the dynamics inherent in good practice in the accreditation of prior learning.

Chapter 7

Example of Good Practice Portfolio: From Management Charter Initiative (MCI)

INTRODUCTION

The last two chapters of this book will contain examples which have been taken from actual portfolios. This chapter will concentrate on a sample from a portfolio submitted for a national vocational qualification (NVQ) level 4.

The examples provided in this chapter represent practice current at the time. The authors and providers of these examples are aware a number of changes have already taken place in the field of competency assessment. The examples remain a useful reflection of APL assessment issues of that period.

STANDARDS

The Management Charter Initiative (MCI) lays down very clear standards against which evidence must be submitted and assessed. The standards are prescribed for NVQ levels 3 to 5 against four key roles:

(1) Manage Operations
(2) Manage Finance
(3) Manage People
(4) Manage Information.

These are further subdivided into units of competences as shown in Table 7. Each unit is then broken down into elements as shown in Table 8. These standards represent agreed best practice in performance of the generic management function.

MCI consulted with sections of industry, commerce and academic institutes in order to define the expected standards of behaviour and underpinning knowledge and understanding of best management practice.

In order to cope with the wide contexts within which the generic standards are expected to operate, ranges of situations are defined.

Candidates are, therefore, able to contextualise and interpret the standards in a unique way while retaining an assessment common ground. The standards fulfil two roles; firstly, generic questions for candidates and organisations and secondly, the yardstick against which assessed decision can be made. This is fundamentally summed up within the Kolb and Fry experiential learning model upon which the principles of the MCI methodology are based.

Table 7 *Occupational standards for manager (Management I) NVQ Level 4 key roles*
Key purpose: to achieve the organisation's objectives and continuously improve its performance

Key role	Units of competence
Manage operations	Maintain and improve service and product operations.
	Contribute to the implementation of change in services, products and systems.
Manage finance	Recommend, monitor and control the use of resources.
Manage people	Contribute to the recruitment and selection of personnel.
	Develop teams, individuals and self to enhance performance.
	Plan, allocate and evaluate work carried out by teams, individuals and self.
	Create, maintain and enhance effective working relationships.
Manage information	Seek, evaluate and organise information for action.
	Exchange information to solve problems and make decisions.

Table 8 *Occupational standards for manager (Management I) NVQ Level 4 units of competence*
Key purpose: to achieve the organisation's objectives and continuously improve its performance

Unit of competence	Elements of competence
1. Maintain and improve service and product operations.	1.1 Maintain operations to meet quality standards. 1.2 Create and maintain the necessary conditions for productive work.
2. Contribute to the implementation of change in services, products and systems.	2.1 Contribute to the evaluation of proposed changes to services, products and systems. 2.2 Implement and evaluate changes to services, products and systems.
3. Recommend, monitor and control the use of resources.	3.1 Make recommendations for expenditure. 3.2 Monitor and control the use of resources.
4. Contribute to the recruitment and selection of personnel.	4.1 Define future personnel requirements. 4.2 Contribute to the assessment and selection of candidates against team and organisational requirements.
5. Develop teams, individuals and self to enhance performance.	5.1 Develop and improve teams through planning and activities. 5.2 Identify, review and improve development activities for individuals. 5.3 Develop oneself within the job role.
6. Plan, allocate and evaluate work carried out by teams, individuals and self.	6.1 Set and update work objectives for teams and individuals. 6.2 Plan activities and determine work methods to achieve objectives. 6.3 Allocate work and evaluate teams, individuals and self against objectives. 6.4 Provide feedback to teams and individuals on their performance.
7. Create, maintain and enhance effective working relationships.	7.1 Establish and maintain the trust and support of one's subordinates. 7.2 Establish and maintain the trust and support of one's immediate manager. 7.3 Establish and maintain relationships with colleagues. 7.4 Identify and minimise personal conflict. 7.5 Implement disciplinary and grievance procedures. 7.6 Counsel staff.
8. Seek, evaluate and organise information for action.	8.1 Obtain and evaluate information to aid decision-making. 8.2 Record and store information.
9. Exchange information to solve problems and make decisions.	9.1 Lead meetings and group discussions to solve problems and make decisions. 9.2 Contribute to discussions to solve problems and make decisions.

ELEMENT/PERFORMANCE CRITERIA/RANGE INDICATORS

Details of how MCI standards at NVQ level 4 are structured are presented below for specific elements. This has been done to familiarise readers with the standards against which candidates (a) interpret their job roles and (b) submit evidence of their own performance, supporting claims of competence in comparison to the laid down 'best practice'.

Each element has associated with its performance criteria a range of indicators which are to be achieved.

Table 9 shows Element 1.1: 'Maintain operations to meet quality standards'. This element relates to the key role 'Manage Operations' and has performance criteria (listed a to j) and range indicators against which the student must submit evidence.

Tables 10 and 11 provide more advice on the type of information the assessor will ultimately be looking for in the evidence submitted.

These elements are those against which the evidence following is presented, where advice was given and against which final assessment was made. Similar information is shown as follows:

Tables 12 to 14 show Element 2.1: 'Contribute to the evaluation of proposed changes services, products and systems'.

Tables 15 to 17 show Element 6.1: 'Set and update work objectives for teams and individuals'.

Tables 18 to 20 show Element 6.3: 'Allocate work and evaluate teams, individuals and self against objectives'.

At the time of writing the new version of the standards is about to be launched. The principles of personal development remain the same. The structure, types of and sources of evidence, are far more accurately specified within range requirements and the knowledge evidence required. Assessment guidance is specified. There are mandatory units and options from which candidates can select as appropriate to their job role.

Table 9 *Occupational standards for manager (Management I)*
Key purpose: to achieve the organisation's objectives and continuously improve its performance;
Key role: manage operations; Unit 1: maintain and improve service and product operations;
Element 1.1: maintain operations to meet quality standards

Performance criteria	Range indicators
(a) All suppliers for operations are available and meet organisational/departmental requirements.	Operations are all those activities within the manager's line responsibility. Sources of supply (suppliers) are both: • external organisations • internal departments/teams
(b) Operations within the manager's area of responsibility consistently meet design and delivery specifications.	Suppliers are: • material • equipment/technology • financial • sub-contractors/consultants/agency staff • information
(c) Information and advice given to customers is accurate, in line with organisational policy and is within the manager's responsibility.	Specifications relate to: • customer agreements • operational means for meeting agreements • specific functional duties within the organisation
(d) All communications with customers are carried out in a manner, and at a level and pace likely to promote understanding and optimise goodwill.	Quality assurance is through systems which are: • formal • informal
(e) Information about operations which may affect customers is passed to the appropriate people.	Communication with customers is carried out by means of: • correspondence • meetings • telephone conversations
(f) Systems to monitor quantity, quality, cost and time specifications for service/product delivery are fully and correctly implemented and maintained.	Factors which disrupt operations are those affecting: • supply • operational resource • quality of materials
(g) Factors which may cause operations to be disrupted are noted and appropriate measures are taken to minimise their effects.	Corrective actions are consistent with organisational policy and within budgetary constraints.
(h) Corrective actions are implemented without delay and appropriate staff and customers informed of any changes which affect them.	• Note: organisational staffing is covered in Unit 1.4.
(i) Records related to the design and delivery of operations for the manager's area of responsibility are complete, accurate and comply with organisational procedures.	
(j) Recommendations for improving the efficiency of operations are passed on to the appropriate people with minimum delay.	

Table 10 *Assessment guidance (Management I) Element 1.1.*
Source of evidence: performance in the workplace over a period of time

Performance evidence required	Forms of evidence

Evidence must cover all those operations within the area of the manager's responsibility and include the following items from the range:
• suppliers of
  materials
  equipment
  finance
  information
• specifications concerning:
  suppliers
  customer requirements (both external and/or other departments' requirements)
  organisation's requirement and methods
• the delivery of the operation against formal and informal quality assurance systems used in the organisation over a period of no less than 6 months
• communications – external customers and/or other internal departments
• factors causing disruption to the operation
	Outputs and products of performance, direct observation, supporting evidence in the form of witness testimony, questioning and a personal report on actions that have or would be undertaken to achieve the standard.
	
	Some aspects of the range and the contingencies implied in the performance criteria may not be sufficiently demonstrated from performance and its outputs alone. Additional evidence of knowledge and understanding will therefore be required.
	
	This should include knowledge of the factors which may cause disruption and the appropriate contingency measures to deal with them and an understanding of the basic principles and methods relating to resource utilisation and control and quality assurance.

Table 11 *Unit I: maintain and improve service and product operations*
Element 1.1: maintain operations to meet quality standards
Purpose and content is an important category of knowledge and understanding, and the content of this category can be found in the accompanying guidance notes.

Principles and methods relating to	Data relating to
• establishing, defining and reviewing objectives and performance measures • monitoring resource utilisation and costs and analysing efficiency and effectiveness • quality assurance and control • communicating with customers to promote understanding and goodwill	• current processes and outputs of services, products and systems • supply specifications, supply levels and available suppliers • factors which may cause operations to be disrupted and contingency measures to deal with them • customers and their current requirements • potential changes in design and delivery specifications • systems for monitoring quality *N.B. Customer can be either internal or external to the organisation*

Table 12 *Occupational standards for manager (Management I)*
Key purpose: to achieve the organisation's objectives and continuously improve its performance; Key role: manage operations; Unit 2: contribute to the implementation of change in services, products and systems; Element 2.1: contribute to the evaluation of proposed changes to services, products and systems

Performance criteria	Range indicators
(a) Feedback from subordinates, customers and users is assessed and passed on together with a reasoned evaluation to the appropriate people	Proposed changes are received from, and information fed back to: • immediate line manager • specialists • subordinates
(b) Proposals for improvements are passed to the appropriate people with minimum delay	
(c) The advantages and disadvantages of introducing changes are assessed against current operational standards and the information forwarded to the appropriate people	Feedback is gathered: • informally • formally Proposed changes involve: • personnel requirements/team composition • employment/work practices • nature and availability of services and products • quality of services and products • methods to reduce waste • new equipment/technology • work methods Change may have an impact on: • profitability • productivity • quality of service/product • working conditions

Table 13 *Assessment guidance (Management I)*
Unit 2, Element 2.1

Performance evidence required	Forms of evidence

Evidence must cover the following items from the range:
 • evidence of proposed changes made by:
    immediate manager
    specialists
    subordinates
 • evaluation to include the impact of changes on:
    profitability
    productivity
    quality of service/product
    working conditions
    work methods
 • informal and formal feedback to:
    immediate manager
    specialists
    subordinates
	• Performance in the workplace. Supporting evidence in the form of witness testimony from those providing feedback and assessing proposals and a personal report on actions that have been or would be undertaken to achieve the standard.
	
	 • Some aspects of the range may not be demonstrated sufficiently from direct evidence alone. Additional evidence from assignments and projects which indicate knowledge and projects which indicate knowledge and understanding of the principles of assessment and evaluation will therefore be required.

Table 14 *Unit 2: Contribute to the implementation of change in services, products and systems Element 2.1: Contribute to the evaluation of proposed changes to services, products and systems Purpose and context is an important category of knowledge and understanding, and the content of this category can be found in the accompanying guidance notes.*

Principles and methods relating to	Data relating to
• assessing alternatives in area of change • informing and consulting others about problems and proposals and encouraging them to offer ideas and views • communicating proposals for change	• current processes and outputs of services, products and systems identified for change • advantages and disadvantages of changes in the short and long term • people affected by the change and their views • objectives, targets and performance related to change

Table 15 *Occupational standards for manager (Management 1)*
Key purpose: to achieve the organisation's objectives and continuously improve its performance; Key role: manage people; Unit 6: plan, allocate and evaluate work carried out by teams, individuals and self; Element 6.1 set and update work objectives for teams and individuals

Performance criteria	Range indicators
(a) Objectives are clear, accurate, and contain all relevant details including measures of performance (b) Achievement of the objectives is profitable within the set period, given other work commitments (c) Objectives are explained in sufficient detail and in a manner, and at a level and pace appropriate to all the relevant individuals (d) Objectives are updated regularly with the relevant individuals to take account of individual, team and organisation changes (e) Individuals are encouraged to seek clarification of any areas of which they are unsure	Objectives are all operational objectives within the line responsibility of the manager. Objectives apply to teams, individuals and the manager him/herself. Objectives are: • short-term • long-term • single • multiple Setting and updating if objectives involve methods of analysis which are: • quantitative • qualitative Objectives are explained: • verbally • in writing.

Table 16 *Assessment guidance (Management 1) Element 6.1*
Source of evidence: performance as a team leader in the workplace over a period of time.

Performance evidence required	Forms of evidence

Evidence must cover all operations objectives within the line responsibility of the manager and include the following items from the range:
• objectives applying to:
    teams
    individuals
    manager him/herself
• short-term, long-term, single and multiple objectives
• quantitative and qualitative analysis methods used
• verbal and written explanations given
	Products such as relevant documentation. Direct observation, questioning supported by personal report of action undertaken and witness testimony from teams, individuals and line manager.
	
	Some aspects of the range may not be sufficiently demonstrated by performance alone. Additional evidence of knowledge and understanding will therefore be required. This must include the context in which work takes place and the principles and methods relating to: establishing, defining and reviewing objectives and performance measures including project planning, methodology and resource allocation techniques.
	
	Evidence should also include indications of the candidate's ability and flexibility in dealing with different situations and individuals and the principal risks and contingent affecting objectives.

Table 17
Unit 6: plan, allocate and evaluate work carried out by teams, individuals and self
Element 6.1: set and update work objectives for teams and individuals
Purpose and context is an important category of knowledge and understanding, and the content of this category can be found in the accompanying guidance notes.

Principles and methods relating to	Data relating to
• establishing, defining and reviewing objectives and performance measures, including using project planning methodology and resource allocation techniques • defining and allocating responsibilities and authority	• work objectives and related performance measures and success criteria • principal risks and contingent factors affecting objectives

Table 18 *Occupational standards for managers (Management 1)*
Key purpose: to achieve the organisation's objectives and continuously improve its performance;
Key role: manage people; Unit 6: plan, allocate and evaluate work carried out by teams, individuals and self;
Element 6.3 allocate work and evaluate teams, individuals and self against objectives

Performance criteria	Range indicators
(a) Allocations optimise the use of resources and the existing competencies of staff	Objectives are all operational and development objectives within the line responsibility of the manager.
(b) Team and individual responsibilities and limits of authority are clearly defined and recorded where necessary	
(c) Where applicable, work activities allocated to individuals provide suitable learning opportunities for the objectives identified in their development plans	Objectives apply during: • induction • projects • normal working
(d) Sufficient information is provided in a manner and at a level and pace appropriate to the individuals concerned, and they are encouraged to seek clarification of their allocated activities	Allocations are made to: • teams • individuals • self
(e) Individuals have appropriate access to, and are supervised by, the people best able to satisfy their agreed work and development needs	Operational and developmental objectives are: • short-term • long-term
(f) Calculations are of a type and accuracy appropriate to the scale and importance of the work being allocated and evaluated	• single • multiple
(g) Where allocations prove to be untenable or unrealistic or organisational demands change, adjustments minimise impact on time and cost	Information is given: • verbally • in writing
(h) Previous allocations are evaluated and used to improve current practice	Calculations are concerned with: • time • cost • criticality

Table 19 *Assessment guidance (Management I)*
Element 6.3

Performance evidence required	Forms of evidence

Evidence must cover all operational objectives within the line responsibility of the manager and include the following items from the range:
• objectives apply during:
    induction
    projects
    normal working
• allocations made to:
    teams
    individuals
    self
• short-term, long-term, single and multiple objectives
• verbal and written information is given
• calculations used concerning time, cost and criticality
	Personal report detailing actions undertaken and what would be undertaken in differing situations, witness testimony from subordinates and line managers, documentation and reports relating to work allocations.
	
	If necessary, questioning will be required to provide additional evidence of flexibility and clarity in:
	• dealing with and motivating staff
	• using different styles of direction and supervision
	• coping with changing situations

Table 20

Unit 6: plan, allocate and evaluate work carried out by teams, individuals and self
Element 6.3: allocate work and evaluate teams, individuals and self against objectives
Purpose and context is an important category of knowledge and understanding, and the context of this category can be found in the accompanying guidance notes.

Principles and methods relating to	Data relating to
• establishing, defining and reviewing objectives and performance measures • motivating staff to reach work objectives through encouraging participation in setting them and using different styles of direction and supervision • identifying, defining and assessing the competencies of individuals • learning and skill development	• resources available to meet objectives • competencies and work preferences of individuals • responsibility and authority limits of individuals and teams • work and project plans, schedules and time-scales • performance of teams and individuals during previous work allocations

CROSS REFERENCING – UNIT/ELEMENTS

In compiling evidence for the portfolio, a student may find evidence which relates to more than one unit or element.

To ensure a student does not have to duplicate evidence a cross referencing system is completed.

An example of such active cross referencing is given in Figure 9.

Here a number and description is given to each piece of evidence and it can be seen that:
01 P. Report – Service Plan has evidence which relates to the unit/elements of 1.1, 2.1, 2.2, 6.1, 8.1, 9.3.

Whereas:

02 Service Plan is evidence which relates to the unit/elements of 1.1, 1.2, 2.1, 2.2, 5.1, 5.2, 6.1, 6.4, 8.1, 8.2, 9.1, 9.3.

Evidence cross reference summary

No	Description	1.1	1.2	2.1	2.2	3.1	3.2	4.1	4.2	5.1	5.2	5.3	6.1	6.2	6.3	6.4	7.1	7.2	7.3	7.4	7.5	7.6	8.1	8.2	9.1	9.2	9.3
01	P. report – Service plan	I	I	I	I								I														I
02	Service plan	I	I	I	I					I	I		I										I	I	I		I
03	Monitoring data	I														I							I	I			
04	Draft service contract	I														I											
05	Service contract	I																									
06	Code of practice	I		I																				I			I
07	P. report – quality	I											I		I												
08	Work brief	I					I						I														
09	Section work prog	I									I		I	I	I				I				I	I			I
10	Individual work prog	I											I		I								I		I		
11	Monitoring form	I																									
12	Letter to supplier	I																									
13	Conser. com. memo	I																									
14	Quality control form	I																									
15	Time monitoring form	I																									
16	Customer questionnaire	I											I														
17	T.S. monitoring data	I																									
18	Customers' letters	I																									
19	P. report – accommodation		I											I													
20	Accommodation photos		I																								
21	Floor plans		I																								
22	H&S audit		I																								
23	P. report – H&S audit		I																								
24	Risk assessment		I																								

Figure 9 M.C.I. candidate's example – NVQ Level 4

The evidence cross referencing summary ensures that evidence can be assessed against a number of units and elements.

Furthermore, it encourages candidates to think holistically about that role. Every task and action will inevitably impact upon different key role areas and, in turn, differing units and elements defining best practice.

In this way the candidate is required to consider, in some depth, the interrelationships of actions and subsequently analyse and reflect upon them. The analyses and reflection is fundamental to the learning process and allows the assessor to establish the depth and breadth of the candidate's appreciation of the management role, ability to contextualise the process and make reference and comment against relevant academic management models and theories.

It will also be noticed that reference is made to 'personal competencies' with examples of the candidate's portfolio. This is a behaviour model describing feelings and motives behind actions. This model complements and enhances the functional model as described with unit/element/performance criteria and provides the candidate with leading questions upon which to base reflective comment. 'It's not what you say – it's the way you say it' could be a description of functional and behavioural models used.

CROSS REFERENCING – PERFORMANCE CRITERIA

In a similar way the evidence can be cross referenced to the performance criteria.

Figure 10 shows that for Unit 1 Element 1, 'Maintain operations to meet quality standards', Evidence 01 P Report – Service Plan related to all the performance criteria (A-J), whereas 02 Service Plan relates only to the performance criteria A, C, D, E, F and I. Figure 11, however, shows the same evidence when cross referenced to Unit 6 Element 1, 'Set and update work objectives for teams and individuals', where Evidence 01 P Report – Service Plan relates to all the performance criteria (A-E) as does the 02 Service Plan.

Unit title: maintain and improve service and product operations; Element of competence: 1.1;
Element title: maintain operations to meet quality standards

Evidence		Performance criteria									
No.	Description	A	B	C	D	E	F	G	H	I	J
01	P. report – service plan	–	–	–	–	–	–	–	–	–	–
02	Service plan	–		–	–	–	–			–	
03	Monitoring data			–		–				–	
04	Draft service contract	–		–	–	–					
05	Service contract	–		–	–	–					
06	Code of practice	–		–	–	–	–	–			–
07	P. report – quality	–	–	–	–	–	–	–	–	–	
08	Work brief	–	–		–		–			–	
09	Section work programme	–	–	–			–	–		–	
10	Individual work programme		–				–	–		–	
11	Monitoring form			–	–			–	–	–	
12	Letter to supplier				–		–	–			–
13	Conservation cmmtt. memo	–		–	–	–		–			–
14	Quality control form		–			–				–	
15	Time monitoring form			–		–				–	
16	Customer questionnaire	–	–	–	–		–	–			–
17	T. S. monitoring data				–		–			–	
18	Customers' letters	–	–	–	–	–					

Figure 10 *M.C.I. Candidate's example – NVQ Level 4. Evidence cross reference form*

Unit no: 6; Unit title: plan, allocate and evaluate work carried out by teams, individuals and self; Element of competence: 6.1; Element title: set and update work objectives for teams and individuals

Evidence		Performance criteria						
No.	Description	A	B	C	D	E		
01	P. report – service plan	–	–	–	–	–		
02	Service plan	–	–	–	–	–		
07	P. report – quality assurance	–	–	–		–		
08	Work brief form	–	–	–	–	–		
09	Tech. work chart		–	–	–			
10	Individual work programme	–	–	–	–	–		
16	Cust. sat. questionnaire	–	–	–		–		
95	P. report	–	–	–	–	–		
131	P. report I.P.D.R.		–	–	–	–		
132	Personal development 93/94	–	–	–	–	–		
133	I.P.D.R. 94/95	–	–	–	–	–		

Figure 11 *M.C.I. candidate's example – NVQ Level 4. Evidence cross reference form*

EXAMPLES OF EVIDENCE

The Personal Report

The following section which has been numbered separately (candidate/Advisor/Assessor example i–xxiv) shows a variety of evidence which has been submitted.

The student has provided a personal report which gives the background to the evidence which is cross referenced to the units/elements and performance criteria (examples i and ii).

There is a front page lead statement into this section of the portfolio to assist in sign-posting the assessor (example i).

This is one particular method of writing and presenting evidence of competence, its key features being clarity and position of claims relative to the narrative and clarity of evidence references within the text. While competence claims are relevant to narrative as a general rule, it is the evidence itself which provides proof of performance. The quality of this evidence and skill in providing contexture narrative (glue binding together evidence) are both vital features of a good portfolio.

Candidates have to be encouraged to present evidence to support their claims to competence in a professional manner but also in a format which facilitates assessment and verification processes. It is therefore important that candidates receive proper advice from suitably trained and qualified personnel (Advisors or Mentors) on an ongoing basis. The learning curve for many is very steep, not only in terms of understanding the standards but the whole concept of searching out evidence and presenting it within a report capturing reflective and understanding concepts. Prompt and frequent contact with candidates within the early stages of the NVQ programme is vital.

Candidate Example (i)

KEY ROLE: MANAGE OPERATIONS

Unit 1: Maintain and Improve Service and Product Operations

Element 1.1: Maintain operations to meet quality standards

To demonstrate my competence within this area of my work, my roles and responsibilities are outlined in the following:

Personal Report – Service Plan
               – Customer Contract
               – Code of Practice

Personal Report – Quality Process

N.B. See also Personal Report Evidence No. 31 (Supply and Control of Resources) Element 1.2. This report also provides prime evidence for Element 1.1 and meets the Performance Criteria A, B, C, E, F and G.

Candidate Example (ii)

Evidence No 7   May 1994

PERSONAL REPORT – A QUALITY PROCESS

The Background:

In 1992 during the Authority and Departmental reorganisation, Technical Support became a separate Service Area. It was necessary to identify and implement several procedures to ensure a team approach to work and customers.

    A consistent approach to quality and its control was required, therefore I introduced and, together with the team over a period of time, implemented the quality control and monitoring procedure described in this report.

The Process: (see Flowchart)

I firstly identified, from experience, the separate stages of the work process and the associated paperwork that would be required.

    The stages in the process were identified as:

6.1a • obtaining customer requirements
       • matching the skills, expertise and knowledge of the technical officer to the task
       • the technical officer applying best practice during the task
       • weekly work programme meetings (between myself and individual officers)
       • customer and technical officer checking the work on completion of Technical Support input
       • customer response to the product and service when the work was completed.

I identified that the paperwork would have to include work briefs and quality control forms, together with a customer satisfaction questionnaire.

6.1e   I discussed the proposed procedure with the team at a team meeting and the idea
1.1e   was actually taken on board and developed by the team during the Nottingham

Candidate Example (ii) *(contd.)*

6.1c,e   into the Nineties training sessions on 'Commitment to Quality' and 'What do our Customers Expect and Want?'.

1.1e   I informed my line manager (John Lynch, Assistant Director – Planning) of the proposed procedure and its implementation at our weekly meeting.

I drafted the paperwork and circulated it around the team for comments. The forms were finalised and Technical Officers within the team designed and produced them.

The procedure is as follows:

(See Evidence No. 08 – Work Brief Form) (1.1abdfi, 6.1abce, 6.3b)

All work requests are supported by a completed work brief. The brief may be completed independently by the customer, or by myself and the customer jointly at a meeting (usually for large and complex projects), or by any member of technical support (usually when the customer gives details of the work required by telephone).

The work brief clearly identifies the customer's requirements, time scales and budget codes. It is at this stage of development of the brief that the customer requires the greatest advice and guidance. (6.3d)

It is my responsibility as the Service Manager to evaluate the customer's request, identify possible problem areas, offer alternatives (where necessary) and ensure sufficient resources are available to be able to carry out work within the required time scales. (6.1b, 6.3a)

(See Evidence No. 09 – Technical Support Work Programme and Chart) (1.1abcefi, 6.1bcd)

Once I am satisfied that sufficient information has been obtained for the work to be started on the project, I enter the project on Technical Support's work programme. The work brief and the detailed planning of the section's work programme ensures that work consistently meets design and delivery specifications.

Using information to identify skills and resources required together with the project deadline, I allocate the work to a particular Technical Officer. (6.3acf)

(See Evidence No. 10 – Individual Work Programme) (1.1befi, 6.1abcde, 6.3be)

The project is then fed into the work programme of one of the Technical Officers. Each officer is responsible for the management of their individual programme, which is used to monitor the progress of projects, identify the release of resources and problem areas, which are discussed at the officer's weekly work programme meeting.

(See Evidence No. 11 – Project Monitoring Form) (1.1 cdeghi, 6.3b)

Throughout the project programme, the Technical Officer records any problems that have been identified and the actions taken, on the monitoring form. This ensures that with complex and problematical projects an objective overview can be obtained. I use the information on the form to debrief Assistant Directors regarding the progress of any particularly time-consuming project. The form clearly identifies the cause of any delay – even that brought about by the customer. The officer works closely with the customer, keeping the customer informed of the progress and any decisions that have had to be taken to keep the project on course – this ensures good customer relations. (6.3e)

Where problems arise, the Technical Officer takes the relevant actions to bring the situation back on line and minimise the effects on the project. Where the supplier is not providing the agreed quality of materials or service, the problem can usually be resolved by the technical officer – with a telephone call to the supplier. This may include either agreeing another supply date or negotiating within the framework of the Authority's financial regulations. (6.3b)

(See Evidence No. 12 – Letters to Suppliers (1.1efghj, 6.3bef, 6.1e)

In the event of circumstances arising that are beyond the control or expertise of the Technical Officer (e.g. suppliers not meeting the target/quality required) – I am notified of the situations, either immediately (depending on the urgency) or at our weekly work programme meetings.

Sometimes it may be necessary for me to write to the supplier – if the problem is complex or if poor practice is liable to have further impact on the quality of the service provided by Technical Support.

Candidate Example (ii) *(contd.)*

The action I take obviously depends on the success of the initial negotiations carried out by the officer and all relevant circumstances must be taken into account.

If the customer has been involved or is aware of the problems I inform them of the actions I and the team have taken and the end result. Contingency plans are also agreed with the Technical Officer to minimise the effect on the project.

(See Evidence No. 13 – Conservation Committee Memo) (1.1acdeghj)
Sometimes it can be other internal services that actually restrict Technical Support from carrying out its work in an efficient manner. The Technical Officers inform me of any such problems in the same way as problems with external suppliers and they deal with the problems, informing me of action they have taken.

Often many problems that arise which require my input can be resolved by an informal telephone call to the other party but, on occasion, it is necessary for me to write to the Service Manager of particular Service Areas, in order to resolve problems and reduce the effect on the operations of Technical Support. (6.3g)

(See Evidence No. 14 – Quality Control Form) (1.1bdfi, 6.3b)
When Technical Support input has been completed on the project, the customer and the Technical Officer complete the quality control form – this is an informal quality control system.

This stage of the process allows the Project Officer to take a step back from the work and obtain another officer's professional assessment. This form also acts as a reminder to the customer that this is the last opportunity, for any customer amendments and alterations after this stage will result in additional costs. (6.3e)

(See Evidence No. 15 – Time Monitoring) (1.1cefi)
On the completion of the project work, the time taken to carry out the work is recorded by the officer in the time monitoring file. As Technical Support does not actually recharge for its work the time recording is a method of monitoring the potential overall cost of a project. This information is also used to monitor the utilisation of the sections time by Service Area, which is supplied to the Departmental Policy and Management Group.

(See Evidence No. 16 – Customer Satisfaction Questionnaire) (1.1abcdefghj, 6.1abce)
Large and complex projects together with a random selection of smaller projects are concluded with the completion by the customer of a Customer Satisfaction Questionnaire.

I evaluate the customer response and identify what actions should be taken to reduce the risk of the problems (identified by the customer) re-occurring in the future. The customer response is also discussed with the lead officer on the project and the customer is informed of the future actions to be taken. Any learning experience is also briefed out at the team meetings by the officer. (6.3h)

(See Evidence No. 17 – Monitoring Data – Technical Support Records)

(See Evidence No. 03 – Monitoring Data – Business Analyst Data) (1.1dfgij)
I monitor the questionnaires monthly, and chase outstanding returns and forward the relevant data to the Departmental Business Analyst who collates the responses for the Department's Policy and Management Group and the relevant Committees.

(See Evidence No. 02 – Service Plan) (1.1bcdefi)
'To continue to monitor and improve customer satisfaction with the service offered' is one objective under the Marketing, Quality and Customer Care section of the Service Plan.

The Customer Satisfaction Questionnaire is therefore one part of a system which is used to obtain this objective, and the progress is monitored by the Performance Indicators.

(See Evidence No. 18 – Customer Letters of Support) (1.1abcde)
Assistant Director and Service Manager
Some customers are actually so pleased with the service they receive from the section that they write to either myself or directly to the lead officer; this is usually before the satisfaction questionnaire is sent out.

Candidate Example (ii) *(contd.)*

Knowledge and Understanding

(Personal Competence)

Reflections on Actions Taken:

The reorganisation of the Authority and the establishment of the section provided the opportunity for improvement. Nottingham into the Nineties training sessions allowed the team to focus on quality through its customers, understanding what the customer required, what was to be achieved by the team and how it could be achieved. (1.1, 2.3, 2.4)

Through Nottingham into the Nineties training (which I carried out myself) and team meetings I was able to introduce the value of customer care and quality control to the team, but I realised that little would be gained from any system introduced, if the team did not help to establish and own the system.

Quality is the key ingredient for any service provider and it is the responsibility of everyone involved in providing the service. This is why I led the initiative yet the team is responsible for its implementation and monitoring and each officer has the authority to take whatever actions are required to ensure its control. Without the team's commitment and ownership, the system would never have worked.

The quality control procedure saves time and money for both the customer and Technical Support; the assurance of quality indicates a consistent operation and gives our customers confidence in the service we provide. The confidence in a job well done also motivates not only the individual officer, but the team.

As an internal service provider it would be easy to take for granted the 'captive customer', but to us the greatest measure of the success of the quality programme operated by our service, is the feedback of customers through questionnaires and letters of support.

Quality Control is built into every aspect of our work – materials used, processes selected, suppliers used, etc. Each officer is encouraged to evaluate each stage of the process, before moving on to the next.

The work brief meeting provides the customer with the opportunity to think through the project in hand and provides in itself a form of quality control, finding out the customer's expectations, before the project proceeds. A few appropriate questions to the customer can alleviate the possibility of many wasted hours of work and customer disappointment. It is often necessary for me to build a complete picture from only a limited amount of information – even on occasion establishing the target audience. (4.1, 4.2)

Many of our customers are not familiar with the processes used in our work and very often it is the first occasion on which they are working on a high profile project that will be seen by the public. It is important that at the work brief meeting with the customer I demonstrate knowledge and understanding of their requirements and confidence in the team's ability to carry out the work. (3.1)

It has become obvious to me from both my experience in providing a service and my personal requirements as a receiver of services that customer loyalty and goodwill is connected with the quality of a service and its product, which in turn promotes the service by the good reputation it acquires. The customer is aware what quality of work will be carried out on their behalf.

All forms of communications with the customer promote understanding and goodwill, when carried out in the correct and appropriate way. Methods available are newsletters, questionnaires (asking the customer what service they require, promoting a positive helpful image), in person and on the telephone, making time for customers; listening to their concerns, responding to requests and giving feedback.

The project monitoring form we use assists in establishing the facts before any decision is taken on a course of action and the quality control form provides both the customer and the Technical Officer with the opportunity of checking all work thoroughly before costly reproduction is carried out.

Candidate Example (ii) *(contd.)*

It is most important to create a climate of support and trust. When a customer feels valued and respected life is pleasanter for both the service provider (us) and the customer. Involving the customer at certain times during the project process can sometimes help them to understand what is actually involved – this can, in turn, highlight to the customer how unrealistic their requests sometimes are and encourages mutual respect.

The Customer Satisfaction Questionnaire was deliberately designed with no leading questions and quick tick responses. This ensured a truthful response and a greater number of returns. The questionnaire is used not only to assess the end product but also our approach to and the management of the project.

I identify positive action required and measure the success of the service from the form. It is also used to measure the quality of the printing and the service provided by external suppliers. Customers' responses to the actual questionnaire are positive; they are pleased that their opinions are valued by us – the service provider – and that they have the opportunity to state if they are not happy with the service.

To attain quality, the section has been prepared to break down existing barriers no matter how difficult, take constructive criticism, put the customer first and take positive action.

The section is committed to its quality procedures and these are reviewed and amended (if necessary) during the quarterly review of the section's Customer Care Programme.

The Planning Process:

The Quality procedure operated by the team was not planned in its entirety; while the basic elements were identified initially, other elements were included as incidents occurred and measures were taken to improve the procedure.

Therefore, the planning process was as follows:

Time Monitoring System introduced	April 1992
Need for Work Brief Form, Quality Control and Customer Questionnaire identified at Nottingham into the Nineties Training	Aug/Sept 1992
Work Brief and Quality Control Forms Implemented Customer Satisfaction Questionnaire included in the 1993/4 Service Plan	October 1992
Weekly Work Programme Meetings Introduced (move into new accommodation made this possible)	February 1993
Need for Project Monitoring Form Identified, form produced and introduced into the procedure	April 1993
Customer Satisfaction Questionnaire produced and implemented	May 1993
Work Brief Form Amended	January 1994
Technical Support Quality Procedure reviewed by the team	April 1994
Quality Control Form Amended as a result of review	May 1994

The Future:

Producing this report has highlighted to me the amount of work Technical Support has already put into improving the quality of its service and products. This report is now to be included within the Sections Procedures Manual and will be reviewed on an annual basis by the team.

Knowledge and Skills Used in this Report:

- Personal Customer Experience, Nottingham into the Nineties Strategy, Customer Requirements/Expectations, Teams' Ideas
- Training, Negotiation, Listening, Investigative, Assessing, Decision-Making, Problem Identifying and Solving.

EXAMPLES OF EVIDENCE (B)

Range of Examples

A range of examples of evidence which relate to the report are contained in the following candidate examples (iii to xiv). The evidence is not shown in its original format which were typical memos, notes, working documents, photographs, etc. either used by the organisation or designed by the candidate to suit operational needs. Some editing has been applied for confidentiality. It is vital that candidates do not produce 'evidence' because it 'looks good' within the portfolio. Raw evidence in its original form is vital for authenticity assessment purposes with suitable comment if necessary where origin may be in question. Any improved or additional documentation or procedure brought about by the NVQ reflective process should be acknowledged within its personal report and supplied and indicated as such.

Evidence is therefore the product of the candidate's everyday work and as such can come in an almost infinite format dependent upon the creativity of the candidate.

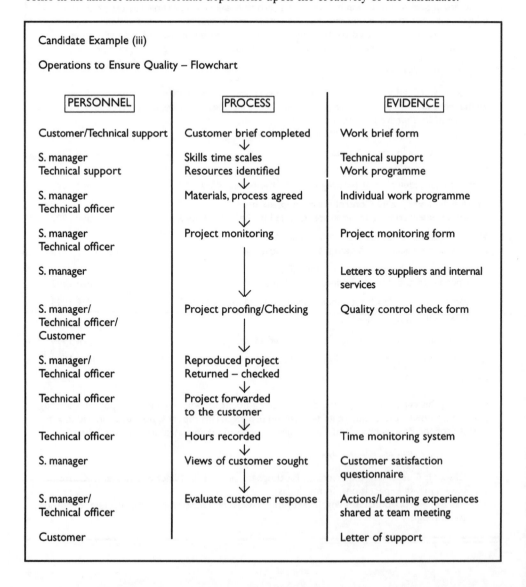

Candidate Example (iii)

Operations to Ensure Quality – Flowchart

PERSONNEL	PROCESS	EVIDENCE
Customer/Technical support	Customer brief completed ↓	Work brief form
S. manager Technical support	Skills time scales Resources identified ↓	Technical support Work programme
S. manager Technical officer	Materials, process agreed ↓	Individual work programme
S. manager Technical officer	Project monitoring	Project monitoring form
S. manager		Letters to suppliers and internal services
S. manager/ Technical officer/ Customer	Project proofing/Checking ↓	Quality control check form
S. manager/ Technical officer	Reproduced project Returned – checked ↓	
Technical officer	Project forwarded to the customer ↓	
Technical officer	Hours recorded ↓	Time monitoring system
S. manager	Views of customer sought ↓	Customer satisfaction questionnaire
S. manager/ Technical officer	Evaluate customer response	Actions/Learning experiences shared at team meeting
Customer		Letter of support

Candidate Example (iv)

Evidence No. 8 *Work Brief Form*

Date ....9.5.94...........................

Originator ....B..Stanley........................   Ext No ....

Project Title ....'Snowboard'.Photos......   Deadline ....Wed..18.5.94...........

Detailed Description of Work Required

Snowboard to be photographed
Then photo to be enlarged to A4
The remaining photos – please choose one of each and enlarge to A4
Possible to crop the photos – get rid of edges? 7 photos

Have you supplied all the information required to complete the project?   YES/NO
If no when will the information be complete?

Budget Code: XXXX XXXX
Technical Officer accepting job: M. Hill
Date: 9.5.94

It is essential that Work Briefs are completed for ALL JOBS to ensure they can be entered into the Technical Support work programme.

Evidence No. 8 (ii) *Design Brief: Nottingham City Council/Task Force Publication*

A. Aims of the Publication

1.   Promote the various business support initiatives provided by the Nottingham City Council/Task Force.
2.   Provide an opportunity to illustrate the impact of support on the business.
3.   Outline the key principles of support.
4.   Specify criteria for assessing funds.
5.   Generate additional interest in the initiative.

B. Technical Details

1.   Full Colour.
2.   A4 – Four sides.
3.   Photographs to be included. (4)
4.   Copy to be supplied.
5.   Use City Council and Task Force Logos
6.   Print Run – 2000/3000.

C. Timescale

The publication has to be designed and printed by the end of the financial year.

D. Budget

A budget of £4,000 is available for the whole exercise.

E. Lifespan

1 year–18 months

Candidate Example (v)

Evidence No. 9 *Technical support work programme and chart*

Job title	Date received	Deadline	Officer
1. Shop Security Leaflet Trans + Enq Amends		?	DRL-PMD
2. Shop Security Quest Trans + Enq Amends		Mid Jan	DRL-PMD
3. Security Certificates		14.1.93	DRL-RJS
4. Textile Strategy	10.1.93	14.1.93	GM-RJS
5. DWLP Document		Early Feb	CB-PMD
6. Environmental Video		21.1.93	AT-AG
7. Householders' Apps Amends	13.12.93	ASAP	DC-PMD
8. SHOPFRONT Guide			TK-RJS
9. L.M.A. Slides		Feb 94	JM-RJS-PMD
10. Dept. Leaflet Translations and Amends		ASAP	JM-RJS
11. Technology Map	14.12.93	ASAP	JA-LC
12. Christmas Lights	14.12.93	ASAP	MJ-AG
13. D.C. Fees Amendments	15.12.93	ASAP	BH-PMD
14. Technology Strategy Maps	15.12.93	7.1.94	JA-LC
15. Ward Boundaries Map	20.12.93	Jan 94	GG-AG
16. Fashion Centre Leaflet	20.12.93	Mid Jan 94	BS-RJS
17. Ashforth St. Brief Amends	21.12.93	11 Jan 94	IV-PMD
18. Ashforth St. Leaflet + Boards	21.12.93	31.1.94 8.1.94	IV-LC
19. River Leen Interpretation Panels	4.01.94		MF-RJS
20. Dept, Poster		ASAP	JM-RJS
21. Mill St Brief	11.01.94	ASAP	MF-PMD-RJS
22. East/West Links	11.01.94	25.01.94	APJ-LC/TR
23. Adams Bldg Feasibility Study	10.01.94	21.01.94	JF-AG
24. Adams Bldg Plans	10.01.94	20.01.94	JF-AG
25. Car Park Signs	23.12.93	ASAP	MG-PMD
26. Dept. Folders		ASAP	
27. River Leen Interpretation Panels	10.01.94	March 94	MA
28. St. Anns Neighbourhood Feasibility Study	11.01.94	ASAP	AT-RJS

SASCO STAFF PLANNER 1994
Photograph of above planner supplied and attached to this evidence.

Candidate Example (vi)

Evidence No. 10 *Individual work programme*

Officer ..M..Hill...

Date ....April..1994..................................

Job	Deadline	Complete	Reasons	M	T	W	T	F	Total
wk. beg 4.4.94									
LMA set up Browne's	6.4.94	6.4.94				1.5			1.5
Tech Weekly Review	6.4.94	6.4.94				0.5			0.5
1. DWLP exhibition (main)	6.4.94	6.4.94				6	9	8.5	23.5
wk. beg 11.4.94									
Set up DWLP Vic Centre	11.4.94	11.4.94		1.5					1.5
2. Planning Comm Studies	14.4.94	14.4.94		6	1	1.75	0.5		
PMD Weekly					1				
TR Briefing MH					0.5				
Tech Weekly Review						0.5			
3. River Leen – MO Aswat						0.25			
SAC Meeting						0.5			
Setting up of equipment for week	15.4.94	15.4.94			0.75	1	0.5	1	
4. LMA Sort Material	15.4.94	15.4.94			5				
5. Take slides for JFT	13.4.94	13.4.94				0.75			

Candidate Example (vii)

Evidence No. 11 *Project monitoring form*

Nottingham Technical Support

Job Dat Project .....TASK FORCE LEAFLET

Production Officer ....R. Stanesby............   Originator ....R. Aujla.......................

Brief Received ....20.2.94..........................   Deadline ....ASAP.......................

Relevant	Comments/Problems	Action
25.2.94	Mock up complete, sent to RA awaiting comments.	
3.3.94	Meeting with Resham – layout of leaflet not what was required – Although brief was strictly followed and mock-up based on an idea which was followed by RA and taskforce.	
9.3.94	Meeting with Resham – new ideas discussed agreed to re-do mock up.	
26.3.94	New mock up complete.	
6.4.94	Task Force not happy with new mock up – want text enlarging – RJS explained that this was not a simple change and it would unbalance the layout and it would need re-designing RJS explained deadline would not be met.	
20.4.94	Task Force leaflet was shelved. P. Burgess has talk with task force and agreed to cut text and job to be kept in house programmed for WB 9.5.94 deadline end of May – out by June.	
13.5.94	Artwork complete.	
13.5.94	To printers.	

Candidate Example (viii)

Evidence No. 12 *Letter to suppliers*

28th April 1994

Dear Mr

I am writing in response to our telephone conversation 27th April 1994 confirming the steps you agreed would be put into practice immediately by your company.

1. All invoices issued by the company will be cross referenced with the Development Department's Official Order Number.
2. The company will respond within 24 hours to all queries made by the Development Department regarding invoices.
3. The company will inform the finance company of any delay in 2 above.
   (This will avoid the situation recurring – where the Development Department is being threatened with Legal action by the finance company – when the delay in payment is actually due to slow response from yourselves.)
4. All invoices should be checked for accuracy before being issued.
5. All work delivered is supported with the delivery note including the relevant order number.

As you are aware I have also discussed these issues with Mr Thompson of the finance company who has also agreed to ensure invoices are supported by an order number.

I am sure you will agree this will save us a great deal of time and bother.

Yours sincerely

Mrs P Davis
Service Manager – Technical Support

Candidate Example (ix)

Evidence No. 13 *Conservation committee memo*

MEMO

FROM: PATRICIA DAVIS

TO: MALCOM SHARP
JERRY SPENCER
c.c. John Lynch
14th December 1992

Our Reference: (TS) PAD/KKB
Your Reference:

CONSERVATION COMMITTEE

The Preparation of Committee Agenda (Existing Situation)

1. Jerry Spencer and Malcom Sharp now select items to be included on the agenda.
   – Items can no longer be placed directly on the agenda, without the agreement of the above.
2. The officer attending the committee is not identified until late in the process, resulting on occasion in confusion and lack of guidance for Registration and Technical Support.

Candidate Example (ix) *(contd.)*

Recommendation

1. Jerry Spencer identifies at agenda preparation stage the officer attending committee. Registration is informed and will include this information on the draft agenda.
2. The draft agenda should also include the name of the case officer and previous committee dates.
    - This will aid Technical Support to identify slides already in the system.
3. That the form attached is used for the draft agenda.

Photography (Existing Situation)

1. It was recently agreed by Jerry Spencer and Malcom Sharp that case officers were now responsible for briefing Technical Supporters to ensure adequate/accurate slides are provided for Committee. (This service was previously provided by C & D.)
2. Due to lack of knowledge about, or resistance to, the new system, case officers are not contacting Technical Support.
3. As a consequence inaccurate slides in some cases have been produced, not only wasting Technical Support time, but also resulting in some applications being referred.
4. Committee has stated that it will not consider items without accurate slides.
5. Technical Support combines CAAC photographic requirements with Planning Committee and usually carries out site visits on the Friday and Monday prior to Committee.

Recommendation

1. That all officers involved in CAAC be made aware of their responsibilities (Jerry Spencer/ Malcom Sharp to prepare a note clarifying the situation).
2. That case officers contact Technical Support regarding their photographic requirements, by Thursday, the week prior to Committee.

Site Plans (Existing Situation)

1. Are not prepared for CAAC
    Resulting sometimes in confusion regarding site location.

Recommendation

1. That site plans are produced for CAAC – The 'new' style CAAC will have fewer items and most will go to Planning Committee the following month.
    - Therefore little extra work will be required to service two committees with one set of plans.
    - These will also aid case officers when briefing Technical Support.

Candidate Example (x)

Evidence No. 14 *Quality control form*

Quality Control

PROJECT TITLE: BDI Leaflet
Check List   Tick Action Taken

1)	Final Proof agreed by Originator: Date Sign		RA
2)	Final Proof checked by T.S. (layout, alignment, pagination)	✓	
3)	Corporate Identity adhered to:	✓	RJ Stanesby
4)	Departmental Identity adhered to:	✓	colour logo
5)	Green Charter Implications:	✓	N/A joint venture
6)	Equality requirements covered:	✓	funded by task force
	a) Text Terminology	✓	Macoprint 170g/m^2
	b) Photo Content		
	c) Language/translations		
7)	All relevant logos.	✓	corporate task force
8)	Financial regulations adhered to:	✓	3 quotes
	(3 quotes obtained, order prepared)		Hawthorns/
		✓	Barnes and Humby
9)	Ordnance Survey licence adhered to:	✓	

Candidate Example (xi)

Evidence No. 15 *Time monitoring*

TECHNICAL SUPPORT TIME RECORDING

Budget Control......................................
Expenditure Code...............................
Division: Training and Employment
Section: Business Support

Date	Originator	Job Description	Costs	Time spent	
April 94		Task Force Leaflet Artwork		RJS	17hrs
		+ Mapwork		RJS	15hrs
April 94		Lord Mayor's Award for		RJS	3.75hrs
		Industry Certificates,			1.5hrs
		Handouts, Plaques Exhibition			10hrs
April 94		Business Support Exhibition		RJS	17.5hrs
				PMD	
May 94		Textile Strategy		RJS	15hrs
26.4.94	T.M.	Setting up Equipment		RJS	0.5hrs
27.4.94		Setting up Exhibition for		RJS/AG	3hrs
		LMA for Industry		LC/RJS	2hrs
	RA	Task Tape for Inserts X2		LC	
24.5.94	CH	LMA for Industry – Plaques Cleaning		PMD/RJS	0.75hr each

Candidate Example (xii)

Evidence No. 16 *Customer satisfaction questionnaire*

MEETING YOUR NEEDS

A Questionnaire for Technical Support Group

Dear ....
To help the Technical Support group provide an effective and efficient service we would be grateful if you could complete the following questionnaire as soon as possible.
The results when monitored will provide us with information about how far we are MEETING YOUR NEEDS and the areas of service we may need to improve.

Commitment to Service: Section 1- (please circle answers)
Please answer as honestly as possible from the scale of performance.

1. The Brief – Was your brief fulfilled?

1	2	3	4	5	6	7	8	9	(10)
Not at all				Partly					Fully

2. Communication
a) Initial contact – Was technical support helpful?

1	2	3	4	5	6	7	8	9	(10)
Not helpful				Fairly helpful					Very helpful

b) Were your calls returned?

1	2	3	4	5	6	7	(8)	9	10
Not at all				Partly				Always	

c) Liaison throughout the project.
Were you kept informed of the progress?

1	2	3	4	5	6	7	(8)	9	10
Never				Sometimes				Always	

ii) Were problems (if any) resolved satisfactorily?

1	2	3	4	5	6	7	8	9	(10)
No				Partly					Yes

iii) Were proofs (if required) supplied prior to print/submission?
(Yes)/No

3. Costs/Quotations
Were you happy that financial regulations were adhered to?
(Yes)/No
If No, please explain why

4. Quality
How would you rate the quality of the finished product?

1	2	3	4	5	6	7	8	(9)	10
Poor				Average				Excellent	

If poor, please explain why

5. Was the deadline achieved?
(Yes)/No

6. Would you use Technical Support Group again?
(Yes)/No

7. Additional comments
Everyone who has seen the signs has remarked on their quality and attractiveness. They should look excellent on site.
Thank you for your co-operation in completing this questionnaire.

Patricia Davis (Service Manager)
483500 Ext 5470
Direct Dial 350896

Candidate Example (xiii)

Evidence No. 17 *Monitoring data – technical support records*

Technical Support
PERFORMANCE INDICATOR

Customer Satisfaction Questionnaire – Response 1994/1995

Date	Customer	Returned	Action
April	Resham Aujla Task Force Leaflet	–	Meeting to be held with customer Areas in time scales to be tightened
April	Colin Heffer Lord Mayor's Award Ind Inc Exhibit, Plaque, Cert	–	N/A (no action required)
April	Resham Aujla Business Sup Exhibition		
April	Tim Kellet Shop Front Design Guide	–	N/A
April	Jocelyn Stevens' visit JFT/Tim Kellet	–	N/A
April	Mcrintha Sykes Fashion Centre photo		
April	Ken Mafham DWLP Posters x2 A3		
April	John Stenberg Lightening Display Page A3	–	N/A
	Clare Ward QTI Application	–	N/A
	Bus Flyer A4 Gold Card M. Garrett	–	N/A

Candidate Example (xiv)

Evidence No. 18A *Customer letter of support*

MEMORANDUM

To: Brian Stanley   From: Paul Burgess

Ref: PB/RTC   Date: 27 January 1994

FASHION BROCHURE

Just a few lines to congratulate you on the Fashion Centre Brochure which I think is now a super advertisement for services at the Fashion Centre. I was particularly pleased to note you developed the brochure in partnership with key companies within the city and how you have brought in additional income to what in effect is quite an expensive publication.

I am particularly pleased with the illustrations and graphics and my congratulations go to Patricia Davis and to Rachel Stanesby in the production of this document. I would be most grateful if you could let me have 10 copies for my personal use and I would also suggest you send 10 copies to Jim Taylor.

Paul Burgess
ASSISTANT DIRECTOR

cc: Patricia Davies
        Rachel Stanesby

Evidence No. 18B *Customer letter of support*

MEMO

From: RICHARD JONES   To: PATRICIA DAVIS

                                                  16th November 1993

Our Reference:

Your Reference:

Patricia, I would like to record my thanks and that of the Local Plans team for all the work that your team have done for us over the past four weeks.

As usual the quality of your team's work is of a very high standard and this is very much appreciated by us and senior management.

Thanks again

Richard

Reports for 2.1 & 2.2 with response to formative questions from the advisor

The following candidate examples (xv to xviii) contain the students' reflections on their practice and the new found knowledge which they have gained by considering the management theory.

These relate to Unit/Element 2.1 and demonstrate how the student believes their actions could have been improved with regard to desk top publishing.

Responses are also given to the advisor questions which sought to clarify the advantages and disadvantages of the proposals.

This response is signed by the advisor on 7-6-95. (xix and xx)

Candidate responses xxi and xxii relate to Unit/Element 2.2 where again an initial report is given followed by reflections and finally a response to questions raised by the advisor.

Advisor Examples xix, xx, xxiii show the types of feedback from the advisor. These pages relate only to Units 2 and 6. Each Unit would have comments from the advisor which would need to be addressed by the student as part of the formative assessment prior to the final assessment.

Candidate Example (xv)

KEY ROLE: MANAGE OPERATIONS

Unit 2: Contribute to the implementation of change in services, products and systems.

Element 2.1: Contribute to the evaluation of proposed changes to services, products and systems.

Introduction:

To demonstrate my competence within this area of work, my roles and responsibilities are outlined in the following:

Personal Report – Geographical Information System/Digital Mapping
   (Line Manager and Specialists)
   (New equipment/Technology)
   (Profitability, Productivity, Quality of Service)

Personal Report – Desk Top Publishing
   (Line Manager, Subordinates and Specialists)
   (Nature, availability and quality of services and products)
   (Methods of reducing waste)
   (New equipment/Technology)
   (Profitability, Productivity, Quality of Service and Working conditions)

See also:

   Evidence No. 73 – Personal Report, Policy and Resources
   Evidence No. 74 – Policy and Resources Report
   (Methods of reducing waste, New equipment/Technology)
   Evidence No. 01 – Personal Report, Service Plan
   Evidence No. 02 – Service Plan
   Evidence No. 06 – Code of Practice
   (Nature, availability and quality of services and products)
   Evidence No. 41 – Personal Report, Personnel
   Evidence No. 42 – Witness Testimony
   Evidence No. 44 – (a) Special bids 1994–1995
   (Personal requirements/Team composition)

Candidate Example (xvi)

Evidence No. 66

March 1994

PERSONAL REPORT – DESK TOP PUBLISHING

(nature, availability and quality of services and products; methods to reduce waste, new equipment/technology and work methods)

The Background:

There have been many advances in information technology, especially in the field of graphic design, with the introduction of Desk Top Publishing. As with all new technology I heard how wonderful this tool was; in my experience the reality often does not match the expectations.

The Process:

I had discussions with printers to assess the external market – they confirmed that this was the direction most printers were taking. I also contacted the internal print section who carry out similar artwork production and established that they too were also investigating the possibility of introducing DTP. Additional discussions with computer specialists also gave me the same indicators.

Now it was essential to thoroughly assess the advantages and disadvantages of introducing DTP against existing work methods and standards.

The advantages/drivers of DTP included: (2.1c)

- Quality, improved and consistent – improving the service to customers
- Savings, on artwork production, purchasing, typesetting and printing – staff time, materials, space
- Reduced waste, text generated once instead of twice
- Speed and flexibility; would increase productivity and eventually profitability
- Storage – compact, easily accessible
- Compatibility, with external printers

The disadvantages/resistors included: (2.1c)

- No support service
- Limited training available (on-the-job training)
- Possible initial delays on project deadlines
- Workforce (fear of change)
- Budget constraints

During this period of investigation I informally discussed the value of DTP with my team and my line manager. It must be noted that at this time the prospect of introducing such a change seemed very slim, due to budgetary constraints. (2.1ab)

Even so, my evaluation of the technology made it clear to me that within the next couple of years DTP would be essential in providing the services offered by the team, and when the opportunity arose I proceeded to implement the change from traditional drawing office methods to computerisation.

(See Evidence No. 67 – Personal Report, Unit 2 Element 2.2 – Implementation of DTP System) (2.1abc)
(See Evidence No. 73 – Personal Report, Unit 3 Element 3.1 - Expansion/Change of system) (2.1abc)
(See Evidence No. 74 (a) – Office Tech. sub Report, Unit 3 Element 3.1) (2.1abc)

Candidate Example (xvi) *(contd.)*

Knowledge and Understanding

Reflections on Actions:

Information on systems was becoming obsolete on virtually a weekly basis and the market was flooded with hundreds of systems. It was difficult for me to decide where to start with my evaluation or to build a complete picture.

It was not necessary for me to know all the functions of software at this stage, as the basic function of those systems available enabled me to decide that DTP was the way forward. The Forcefield Analysis would be used later to evaluate each system if the money became available. (4.3)

I was conscious that whilst discussing the possibility of DTP with the team, it was necessary to introduce the change in the best light possible, convey the concept clearly and at a level that was understood by all. For the change to have complete success I needed the commitment of the team, which I gained through regular discussions, linking team and individual goals, allaying fears, and expressing confidence in the new method of working. (1.1 and 2.3)

Good communication was essential in setting the stage for change and whilst many problems were encountered in the implementation and development of the DTP system, the change has always been viewed as a positive move. (2.3)

Knowledge and Skills Used in this Report:

- Corporate Policies, Local Government Management Board, Ordnance Survey Mapping, Map Management

- Negotiation, Communication, Assessment/Evaluation, Research

---

Candidate Example (xvii)

KEY ROLE: MANAGE CHANGE

Unit 2: Contribute to the implementation of change in services, products and systems.

Element 2.2: Implement and evaluate changes to services, products and systems.

Introduction:

To demonstrate my competence in this element I have outlined my roles and responsibilities in the following reports:

- Implementation of Desk Top Publishing System
  (New Work methods, New equipment/Technology, Nature and availability of services and products, Personnel requirements and Methods to reduce waste)
  (Customers, Suppliers and Subordinates)
  (Profitability, Productivity, Working Relationships)

- Time Monitoring System

  (Methods to reduce waste, New technology and work methods)
  (Profitability, Productivity)

See also Prime Evidence No. 41 – Personal Report, Permanent Post and Knowledge and Understanding (Personnel requirements/Team composition)

Candidate Example (xviii)

Evidence No. 67

June 1993

PERSONAL REPORT – IMPLEMENTATION OF DESK TOP PUBLISHING SYSTEM

The Background:

I supervised the team of Planning Technicians which provided a daily support service to the Planning Department. The service included photography and map production, with a growing service in publication production.

I was aware of the new technological developments within the field of Graphic Design, especially Desk Top Publishing, designed specially for the production of documents and leaflets.

I had already evaluated the effect of DTP on the work of the team (see Unit 2, Element 2.1 Personal Report). What had earlier appeared to be desirable, would now over the next few years become an essential tool.

This area of development had to be approached with a certain amount of caution; technology was improving so fast and packages were becoming obsolete overnight.

The Process:

Computerised systems were being introduced to various service areas within the Planning Department; one such service was located within the same room as myself. Over a period of time I negotiated with the officer – David Hemmett developing the computer system, about the possibility of 'bolting' DTP onto the proposed Census package, using the advantages of improved service and reduced costs in producing Census documents to add weight to the argument. (2.2a, 2.1b)

Over a period of time, relevant details of the proposed implementation of DTP were discussed with the rest of the team at the team meetings and my line manager. Their response, whilst apprehensive, was positive and I continued to pursue this line of development. (2.2a, 2.1a)

As the implementation of the main system took place, it was finally agreed by the developing officer, David Hemmett, that DTP would form part of the package, as it would be provided free with the census package, therefore, I was to have no input regarding choice, etc. All the earlier discussions and negotiations had taken place on an informal basis, now it was time to formalise the arrangements and show commitment.

Two Technical Officers were identified, to receive training and work with the package. It was essential now for the team to develop its skills and establish its role in DTP.

A 'booking' system was introduced to eliminate user conflict with the host section, existing information storage systems were modified and transferred onto the computer, together with text generation requirements. All this was in accordance with the implementations plans and the agreed specifications.

(See Evidence No. 68 – Performance/Workload Indicators) (2.2bc, 2.1c)

Changes in the service and products were monitored and evaluated informally by myself. The quality of the documents produced was vastly improved, and at a reduced cost, although limited knowledge and experience initially extended the production time, having an adverse effect on the overall service provided by the team. Traditional production methods that were known and consequently quickly carried out, had been replaced by many unknowns. (2.2bc)

I had expected production to be expanded and was not unduly worried as the situation had been fully briefed to all customers and extended deadlines agreed. The only modification required to resolve the production time extension was to identify those projects where the deadline would allow the learning process to take place. Therefore, the section was operating the new and traditional systems together. (2.2d)

I had informed the print suppliers of the change in our work methods and actively sought to

Candidate Example (xviii) *(contd.)*

identify problems with the printers and the processes they used. A series of tests had to be carried out with the print suppliers to confirm compatibility of equipment and new procedures. (2.1c)

(See Evidence No. 69 – D. Robinson, Witness Testimony) (2.2abcd)

Knowledge and Skills Used in this Report:

- I.T. Development Awareness, Production processes, Customer Requirements
- Negotiation, Communication, Identifying and solving problems, Monitoring, Evaluation

Knowledge and Understanding

(Personal Competence)

Reflections on Actions:

Whilst method of implementation was not ideal and was beyond my total control, it was the only method by which I could obtain a foothold in technological developments. Desk Top Publishing was implemented not as a totally planned process but rather by an opportunity being presented and it being seized by myself.

The host selection, whilst being accommodating, never really acknowledged the skills developed by Technical Support and maintained 'ownership' of the package. This method of implementation allowed the 'water to be tested, before diving in'. It enabled the package to be fully assessed at small cost before large amounts of money were committed. The increased productivity and improved quality was used to gain management support and justify full implementation. (3.1)

It was essential to closely monitor the effects of the change on the service; with no improvement or obvious long-term benefits I would have stopped the process immediately, as this would have been a waste of resources and would have demotivated the team. (4.3)

However, the advantages of the system were soon realised. The team had recently been reduced by two members of staff, yet it was now producing more documents and leaflets than before, reflecting greater productivity and profitability. The service was improved by reduced response times, increased flexibility and expansion into O.H.P/poster and document cover production.

- There was a reduction in the duplication of work, stock wastage (e.g. Letraset) and equipment/tool requirements, saving time and money.
- Working conditions were marginally improved as toxic materials and adhesives were no longer used.
- The response of customers was positive; the demand for this service increased to such an extent that the team now operates two dedicated work stations.

The time scale of this project actually allowed me to introduce the idea of such a vast change over a period of time. I discussed new developments informally with the team and obtained their views and ideas. During these discussions I was able to allay any fears and set out the positive aspects of the change. (2.1, 2.2)

I knew the introduction of a new working method would be easy if the team was optimistic and aware of its advantages. Without the commitment of the team, their input and acceptance of this change, this venture would not have succeeded. (2.3)

Though time-consuming, complex and at times frustrating, tests were essential to us and the suppliers, as all our future work would be based on the findings. This was frightening and exciting at the same time; a problem solved was very rewarding. (4.1)

Candidate Example (xviii) *(contd.)*

The efficiency of the system today is based on the greater understanding of the process, drawn from these discussions.

I had to make time available to support the package operators. We would discuss the problems experienced, but more importantly we would discuss their anxieties. It was essential that they felt their input was of value, to ensure they remained motivated, during this difficult period of adjustment. (2.1)

There were times when the numerous short-term problems sometimes made me wonder if the long-term advantages could ever be realised. My instinct and the results of the initial projects told me to press on, and I am glad we did, as this change was a definite opportunity for improvement. (3.1)

Having investigated the initial stages, I maintained my commitment and confidence in the success of this development, despite the problems experienced. If I had not taken control of the situation and had accepted the status quo, Technical Support would still be operating out-dated work methods. (3.1)

Refer to Knowledge and Understanding, in Element 2.1, for communicating plans to ensure co-operation and informing and consulting others.

The Future:

I have since attended a training course on I.T. Management which has provided me with the knowledge of system identification, training, review, development and modification. Having seen the advantages and disadvantages experienced during DTP implementation, I am approaching future I.T. developments (Digital Mapping and DTP expansion) with more confidence.

FEEDBACK FROM ADVISOR

Lead questions are posed and discussed with the candidate to facilitate understanding of the modifications necessary to the portfolio. This is usually accomplished by a one to one meeting between candidate and advisor, but any form of contact is feasible, dependent upon time, geography and relationship between the parties. Obviously candidates will at least need formative assessment reports copies and possibly return of the portfolio.

Often candidates submit copies of the portfolio entries. Whilst this is costly and time-consuming it precludes undue delay and security problems associated with transportation and/or storage of portfolios. Use of suitable forms of IT will be fruitfully researched in this area.

Additional work is submitted (xxi to xxii) in response to questions. Although not done in this instance, candidates may choose to rewrite reports and include additional/different evidence for consideration.

The process is then iterative, bearing in mind expectation/concern levels of the candidate. Advising processes must be performed with sensitivity but strictness; it is therefore essential that advisors are qualified assessors.

Once the iterative process is complete, the candidate is advised of the situation and the portfolio passed forward for summative assessment and verification.

Advisor Example (xix)

FORM CC7   CANDIDATE REGISTRATION NO.

FORMATIVE
ASSESSMENT OF PORTFOLIO

Candidate   ......PATRICIA DAVIS............   Level   ....MS + NVQ4.....................

Advisor   ....TC RICH..................   Advisor Tel No   ....

Assessor   ....   Date Evidence Received 8.2.95..............

Date of Assessment ..17.2.95..................   Time Taken   ..8.0 hours........................

UNITS CLAIMED   1   **2**   **3**   **4**   **5**   6   7   **8**   **9**

ASSESSOR REPORT:

Unit 2   Evidence of Report

Logical development of arguments, observation of practices and discussions, K & U well illustrated.
Personal competencies well chosen.

Cross-referencing to other units possible – 3; 8; 9 possibly 7

Evidence 66 Report

How were the advantages/disadvantages arrived at?   (Q1)

Evidence 68 Its origins could perhaps be enlarged upon and suitably acknowledged as an authentic document particularly with number of 2.1 and 2.2 claims. Evidence 69 needs to be signed by witness.

Extensive links into other evidence sets relevant to give the balance of the evaluation and processing of the change process.

Range coverage for 2.1 relevant but needs a matrix building up.   (Q2)

Evidence 67 report good personal but evidence 68 could be questioned and performance criteria not really supported with evidence.

Evidence 70 report logically presented but direct evidence is a bit light with extensive pro's claimed just on the basis of the personal report.   (Q3)

DATE ASSESSMENT REPORT CONTINUES OF FORM CC7A: YES/NO

Assessor Signature: ....TC RICH...............   Date: ....18.2.95............................

Page 1..of..9

Advisor Example (xix) *(contd.)*

FORM CC7   CANDIDATE REGISTRATION NO. ....
FORMATIVE
ASSESSMENT OF PORTFOLIO

Candidate ....   Level ....

ASSESSOR REPORT: (Continued)

The extent of range coverage for 2.2 needs to be established. Possible areas to be explored are changes involved: waste; info effects: suppliers; outcomes; working conditions; evaluation qualitative.

General: the aspect of range could be established at the end of each element with the necessary comments to address any gaps on less clear connections.

K&U well established and again personal competence model well used.

Clarification of Q's 1-3 with perhaps some minor additional information should complete unit 2.

Assessor Signature: ....   Date: ....

Page 2..of..9

Advisor Example with Candidate Responses (xx)

FORM CC8
FORMATIVE
ASSESSMENT INTERVIEW PLAN

Candidate ....   Level ....

Advisor ....   Date of Interview   ....

Assessor ....   Units ....

ELEMENT		QUESTION	RESPONSE
2.1	Q1	How did you arrive at the advantages/disadvantages of the change proposals?	See reply in file OK with evidence in 66; 67; 73; 74a TCR 7-6-95
	Q2	What method could you establish for indicating an overview of range coverage across personal reports?	See reply in file range indicators at unit introduction and at each evidence. TCR
2.2	Q3	What sources of evidence could you produce to substantiate claims made in evidence 70 report?	Witness testimony, or observation by advisor.
3.1	Q4	How can you authenticate evidence?	Line manager to sign, see justification in file/OK. TCR 7/6.
	Q5	Can you prepare a brief resume either verbally or written on the actual v/s budget (differential costs) and risk analysis (ROCE) for the 73 evidence.	See K & U in report 73/accepted. TCR 7/6

DATE ASSESSMENT INTERVIEW PLAN (CC8) SENT TO CANDIDATE

Assessor Signature ....   Date ....

Candidate Response (xxi)
Evidence No. 68 (Additional candidate information)

M.C.I. CERTIFICATE IN MANAGEMENT – NVQ LEVEL 4

Evidence Justification   Evidence Title: Performance/Workload Indicators

Prime Units/Elements this Evidence Supports

Unit	Element	Performance Criteria
2	2.2	b, c

Reason/Rationale for Inclusion:

This document was produced from the monthly monitoring information provided by the team.
    Each team member would enter under the relevant section the projects completed the previous month.
    I produced the document for my own interest in the performance of the team, by manually calculating the total of each product.
    (This information is now produced automatically by the Time Monitoring System recently developed.)
    This information is now passed on to my line manager and included in the Service Plan. It has also been used to justify the development of the DTP system further.

Date: 21/2/95

Candidate Response (xxii)

M.C.I. CERTIFICATE IN MANAGEMENT – NVQ LEVEL 4

Response to Advisor Questions re: *P. Report No. 66*

Question 1

'How did you arrive at the advantages/disadvantages of the proposals?'

i)   Identifying what I required from the proposed package – this was achieved by objectively assessing the existing method of production, its limitations and its strengths.
ii)   Gathering sufficient information from reliable sources:
        - external suppliers and other Authorities using the proposed package
        - the team
        - magazine articles, television, etc.
iii) Identifying what would be required to run the proposed package effectively and efficiently:
        - training
        - support
        - funding.
iv)   Identifying the greatest impact of implementation on existing work methods, personnel and products
        (Through ii above).
v)   Evaluation of i – iv drew out advantages/disadvantages together with knock-on effects.
vi)   Long-/short-term advantages/disadvantages assessed. Those which cancelled out in the short term were not listed.
      Long-term advantages/disadvantages were used to justify the new system and identify the areas requiring input.

25/2/95

Candidate Response (xxii) *(contd.)*

Unit 2.1

Question 2

'What method could you establish for indicating an overview of range coverage across the personal reports?'

A portfolio overview could be indicated by the use of a matrix, such as the Evidence Cross Reference Summary Sheet.

A personal report overview could be obtained by the use of matrix, such as the Evidence Cross Reference Form, used for performance criteria reference.

Both these methods would assist the advisor and the assessor, but it would have to be highlighted at the start of portfolio production that this was the required method, to be used by all participants.

The method I have adopted is to show the range each personal report covers on the Element Overview Sheet at the beginning of each element's personal reports.

The range is in brackets, below the title of the report.

25/2/95

Advisor Example (xxiii)

FORM CC7   CANDIDATE REGISTRATION NO.   ....

(for office use only)

ASSESSMENT OF PORTFOLIO

Candidate   ........P.D...   Level   ....Management NVQ4..............

Advisor   ....TCR.................................   Advisor Tel No   ....

Assessor   ....   Date Evidence Received   ....19.5.....

Date of Assessment   ....7.6.....................   Time Taken   ....4.5.........................

UNITS CLAIMED   1   2   3   4   5   6   7   8   9

ASSESSOR REPORT:

6.1 & 6.3	Extensive coverage evident. May need clarification of quantitative/ qualitative issues at interview.
6.2	OK
Unit 7	Evidence relevance and extent of cross referencing impressive. Both units with amendments 6 2, 3, 4, 5, 8, 5 all passed for summative assessment

DATE ASSESSMENT REPORT CONTINUES OF FORM CC7: YES/NO

Assessor Signature: ....TCR...............................   Date: ....7.6..............................

Page 1..of. 1

At this point and before summative assessment is discussed, it is important to highlight the role of advisor to the whole process of portfolio compilation.

The relationship developed between candidate/advisor is vital if the very introverted and self-critical learning process is to proceed.

This is the normal barrier experienced by candidates over and above the other more practical difficulties of writing reports, sourcing evidence, interpreting standards, addressing knowledge gaps by various study methods and generally keeping the staff development process going in addition to life's normal chaos.

The basic difficulties with this portfolio approach, be it by APL or planned development, is that the structure and timetable of events is very fluid. The traditional academic programme perhaps offers more structure but more importantly offers a series of preset 'questions' which candidates address within the framework of formal assessment guidelines and often marking criteria.

The very nature of NVQs in management in particular, is the quite difficult task of directing candidates in a generic sense and helping them ask themselves the right kind of questions. Paradoxically, the candidate has to establish the correct question and then provide a suitable answer. Similarly, the advisor/assessor has to be able to appreciate rather than set the question and furthermore comprehend the context of the answer. All one can really offer candidates is a methodology of structuring, as simply as possible, their own unique portfolio.

Ironically, the advising process is technically outside the verification process as it does not in itself lead to the certification process. The advisors, to quite a large extent, have not had a sufficiently high profile. One only has to assess a portfolio which was badly advised to appreciate the problem. This does not mean all difficult portfolios are the responsibility of the advisor – you can only lead some horses to water! It is for this reason that separation of advising and assessing roles is vital. Sheer frustration or familiarity should be professionally recognised and summative decisions dedicated to a third party. Whether this role is that of assessor or verifier is the argument that the awarding bodies have to come to grips with. The principle is clear.

ASSESSMENT OF PORTFOLIO

Once the advisor is in agreement, the whole portfolio is submitted to an assessor who will check each unit.

The example given shows that the student has successfully supplied evidence to satisfy the performance criteria and range of all nine units.

The queries raised by the advisor with regard to Unit/Elements 6.1 and 6.3 have specifically been checked by the assessor and found to be acceptable. (Assessor Report xxiv)

The candidate included with the finally submitted portfolio details of advisory queries with the relevant responses.

Providing any concerns have been addressed, the portfolio could be updated and the summative assessor have no necessity to know what has happened previously. The portfolio should stand alone. It may well be, as in this example the candidate chose to include advisor/candidate responses to save time and possibly unnecessary rewrites.

Verification of the assessment process would be carried out on a statistical sampling basis, with the verifier viewing all assessment documentation which could well include advisor documentation and the portfolio itself. Interviews or meetings between any of the parties could again be sampled by the verifier to ascertain validity of the decision prior to application for certification.

Relevant Awarding Bodies wish when candidates are originally registered, to carry out a similar Quality Assurance process ensuring all documentation is complete and the decisions are valid and recorded in such a way as to be independently assessable.

All facets of the process are addressed by the candidate and within the portfolio.

Evidence; Content, Performance Criteria, Range, Knowledge must be visible and the Validity, Sufficiency, Reliability, Authenticity, Currency and Confidentiality ensured. Only in this way can one be certain of the quality of the assessment decision-making process which should be reproducible and auditable.

Assessor Report (xxiv)

FORM CC7   CANDIDATE REGISTRATION NO. ....

(for office use only)

ASSESSMENT OF PORTFOLIO

Candidate .......P.D............................   Level ....Management NVQ4.........

Advisor ....TCR............................   Advisor Tel No ....

Assessor ....LK............................   Date Evidence Received ....7.6.......

Date of Assessment ....11.6.........   Time Taken ....6.0...........

UNITS CLAIMED		I	2	3	4	5	6	7	8	9	

ASSESSOR REPORT:

1.1	1.2	2.1	2.2	3.1	3.2	4.1	4.2	5.1	5.2	5.3	6.1	6.2
–	–	–	–	–	–	–	–	–	–	–	–	–
–	–	–	–	–	–	–	–	–	–	–	–	–

6.3	6.4	7.1	7.3	7.4	7.5	7.6	8.1	8.2	9.1	9.2	9.3
–	–	–	–	–	–	–	–	–	–	–	–
–	–	–	–	–	–	–	–	–	–	–	–

An excellent portfolio
Very clearly presented
Personal competence very well addressed

DATE ASSESSMENT REPORT (CC7) SEND TO CANDIDATE:

PORTFOLIO ASSESSMENT REPORT CONTINUES OF FORM CC7A: YES/NO

Assessor Signature: ....LK...

Date: ....11.6...

Page 1 of 3

Assessor Report (xxiv) *(cont.)*

FORM CC7A   CANDIDATE REGISTRATION NO. ....

(for office use only)

ASSESSMENT OF PORTFOLIO

Candidate: ....PD..

Level: ....Management.NVQ4...

ASSESSOR REPORT: (Continued)

The Advisor's formative assessment and subsequent question and answer session has ensured that any minor gaps or areas requiring clarification have been covered.

I have specifically looked at 6.1 and 6.3 re: the advisor's comment on range: quantitative and qualitative and I am happy that these areas of range are covered.

Assessor Signature: ....LK...

Date: ....11.6...

Page 2..of..3

ASSESSMENT OF PORTFOLIO

Is the evidence:	Tick	Comments
VALID	–	
SUFFICIENT	–	see attached
RELIABLE	–	
AUTHENTIC	–	
CURRENCY	–	signed, validated
CONFIDENTIALITY	–	dated

Is there a balance between direct and indirect evidence?
Balance of evidence type presented.
The majority is direct evidence.

Page 3..of..3

While details within this chapter have been derived from a comprehensive APL portfolio by a very literate candidate and almost exclusively paper-based it should not be taken as the only methodology of advising and assessing

There exist many different ways for candidates to amass and present evidence of their competence, ranging from direct observation through simulation to presentation of written work. The vehicles for presentation again ought to be flexible and suitable for the candidate. Paper-based portfolios may suit one candidate, as in our example, but creative use of information technology and audio/visual techniques may be more appealing or appropriate to another. Quite often there may be a combination of methods employed.

Special needs and anti-discriminatory/equal opportunity issues need to be implicitly addressed within the advice and guidance given to candidates.

The one common criterion however is the need for rigour and documentation of the formal or summative assessment process.

1996 has been a significant period of change for NVQs and GNVQs in general, following the Capey (1995), Beaumont (1995) and Dearing (1996) reports, and to MCI in particular as a result of their review of the standards.

Beaumont (1995) studied one hundred NVQs and SVQs in a report for the Department for Education and Employment during 1995. While concluding that NVQs had widespread employer support and that 75 per cent in England, (87 per cent in Scotland), indicated that the benefits outweighed the costs, significant criticisms were made. These included the way standards were written, plain English (Welsh) needing to be introduced, clearer knowledge and understanding specification, fresh guidance and best practice be issued on assessment, use of portfolios and simulation, and that providers make traditional vocational qualifications and professional qualifications outcomes-based and aligned with NVQs/SVQs.

NCVQ (Hillier 1996) have responded by reaffirming their commitment to quality of NVQs and among other comments relative to the Beaumont report are:

> currently engaged in examining the desirability and feasibility of introducing a significant element of *external assessment*. This would mean that part of the assessment decision is independent of the candidate's supervisor or trainer. Research indicates that employers would find this reassuring.

The interpretation of this enquiry by Awarding Bodies and providers is yet to be seen but the principle of independence of assessment to the advising function in order to retain rigour is clearly stated by NCVQ and has already been recommended in this chapter. It would appear more controllable and cost effective if separation of roles is achieved at centre or provider level and that external assessment is maintained by Awarding Bodies to monitor quality assurance methodologies rather than commit themselves to formal and direct candidate assessment.

Notably both the Institute for Personnel and Development (IPD) and the National Examining Board for Supervision and Management (NEBS Management), City & Guilds' management wing, are both staunch advocates of the separation of advisor–assessor–internal verifier roles in respect of any one individual candidate.

MCI are currently undertaking a comprehensive review of the management standards. As these standards are integrally part of a great many other qualifications structures, for example TDLB's 1994 NVQ levels 3 and 4 (both Learning Development and HRD) contain appropriate management standard options. At the time of writing, the revised standards have yet to be issued but pilot work undertaken would point to a significant overhaul and restructuring. Introduction of probable core and options at each of levels 3, 4 and 5, language simplification, clearer evidence and underpinning knowledge specifications and guidance to assessors will bring them in line with the structure of many other standards.

Chapter 8

Modular Degree APL Portfolio

INTRODUCTION

This chapter presents an APL portfolio submitted against a modular degree programme (BSc Horticulture). The portfolio represents accredited modules relating to industrial placement. The candidate had already mastered the learning outcomes of this placement and as such was seeking exemption through the submission of this portfolio. As stated in the introduction the purpose of this chapter is to demonstrate good practice in relation to the maintenance of institutional quality assurance.

The portfolio was much larger than the space available here. What is presented here is therefore an abridged version of the entire portfolio. There are references to the portfolio's Appendices that are not reproduced here. However, the references have been retained as an example of the depth of evidence required.

Issues to note

Areas of particular note within the portfolio are:

* Evidence of organisational documentation in which the role of the advisor, assessor and verifier is indicated (progress and approval form).
* The applicant's evidence combines qualitative and quantitative evidence. The student also gives reflective narrative of what was learnt. In this way the portfolio not only demonstrates mastery of subject content and knowledge but also indicates the generic intellectual analytical skills.

The portfolio was submitted to the APL Committee for their consideration.

* The portfolio, together with the organisational document (progress and approval form) was submitted to a college-wide APL Committee. The primary purpose of this is to act as a quality assurance mechanism in terms of ensuring equity of judgement and standards across the different subject-fields within the modular scheme.

A report written by a member of the group is enclosed. A further quality assurance strategy generated within the college would be to make available all submitted portfolios, together with supportive/administrative documentation to a designated external verifier; again to ensure equity and transparent quality.

Purpose of APL Committee is to act as APL quality assurance committee to ensure:

* that the objectives and learning outcomes of the modular scheme are being attained;
* that standards of attainment are comparable to similar programmes elsewhere;
* that equity and fairness is being maintained;
* that good practice in the accreditation of prior learning prevails.

REVIEW OF PORTFOLIO

College wide: APL portfolio review committee

The portfolio was reviewed by three members of the committee and the following determined:

- To confirm the award of credits as recommended by the assessor.
- There was evidence of verification within the supportive administrative documentation.
- The portfolio did seek to match appropriately the given learning requirements associated with the case to the candidate; prior learning supported by a range of evidence.
- The portfolio and associated academic judgements underpinning the accreditation was comparable to other portfolios submitted in this field and others within the modular degree scheme.

Industrial placement period

1. The purpose of the industrial placement is:
    - to provide an opportunity for you to apply knowledge and skills acquired during the early part of your course
    - to provide you with an opportunity to develop competency in the application of some of your skills
    - to develop a foundation of practical knowledge and experience on which the student group as a whole can draw in studies in the final stages of the course
    - to develop a deeper insight into the operation of the industry and a sensitivity for the interpersonal relationships involved
    - to improve your understanding of the industry so that you are able to make informed decisions on career plans.

2. To assist in the achievement of these aims, during the industrial placement you will:
    - develop an understanding of the range of work activities carried out by organisations operating in the horticultural industry
    - identify the objectives of the various parties involved in horticulture
    - identify the management structures and policy making processes of your employer
    - submit assignments to college supervisors.

3. On conclusion of the placement period it is expected that you will be able to:
    - carry out horticultural and technical skills associated with the specialist 'enterprise' in which you have been involved
    - prepare a critical account of the full range of operations in which the enterprise is involved having seen or been exposed to as wide a range as possible
    - work in a team towards an enterprise goal
    - prepare a report on a specialist aspect of an enterprise in which you have been involved. Look at the subject in an integrated or research way so that the results can be used to the advantage of the 'enterprise'
    - take responsibility for a small part of the operation of the enterprise
    - make decisions on a technical and management basis

- discuss with senior management aspects of business and the running of the business enterprise
- develop life skills associated with the workplace.

4. Responsibility for the placement of students is divided between the Course Director of Studies, the Assistant Course Manager(s) and the Pershore College's Placement Co-ordinator. The Assistant Course Manager(s) will interview each student to ascertain the individual's needs and interests. Then, in consultation with the Placement Co-ordinator, suitable opportunities will be identified. Employer interview(s) will then be arranged in accordance with the College's policy on industrial placements.

5. Students will normally have practical experience in the horticultural industry over 48 weeks in the Industrial Placement Period. This continuous placement is usually preferred by employers to two shorter periods or other fragmented experience possibilities.

   This does not rule out the possibility for two six-month placements if it meets with the specific requirements of the student or if the cycle of work in specialist enterprises is of such a nature that students will benefit from the shorter work experience pattern.

6. Each student will maintain contact with the College via a member of the course team acting as Placement Tutor. Again in accordance with the College's policy on placement supervision, tutors will visit students soon after the start of their placements to check on progress and to provide counselling and guidance as required. Contact may be maintained and feedback achieved by further visits, telephone, or letter/facsimile as appropriate.

7. During the placement you will be required to produce a placement report covering the following specification:

   i) an analytical account of the employing organisation, including its objectives, function, structure, range of work and relationships with other organisations;
   ii) an account of a project being undertaken by the organisation with which you are involved. Alternatively, and where appropriate, it may be a report on a smaller project which is your direct responsibility and which is carried out to satisfy a particular requirement of the employer. The choice of project, the extent of student involvement and matters of business confidentiality will be discussed with the placement tutor and the employer during the first visit. Example activities which would fulfil the requirements of this exercise might include:

   - an evaluation and detailed account of a selected crop grown on the holding
   - the assessment of visitor potential to a garden centre business
   - an appraisal of the management of a landscape contract project
   - the development of a maintenance schedule for an area of amenity/recreational grounds
   - the aims, methodology and results of a piece of research and development work.

8. The first part of the assignment will carry 30% of the marks for the written assessment – the remaining 70% being attributed to a second part. The student's qualities as an employee will be assessed by the employer in discussion with the Placement Tutor. This assessment will be concerned with items such as interpersonal skills, organisation, conscientiousness and reliability. A structured questionnaire will be used in this exercise to

improve objectivity. Following completion of the questionnaire, the Placement Tutor will extract an overall rating of the student's performance as an employee which will be included as part of the student's overall Graded transcript/Notification of Performance.

9. Some students may enter the course after experience in the horticultural industry. The Course Team recognises that in suitable cases, the Accreditation of Prior Learning (APL) could be used as the basis for exemption from the Industrial Placement Period. In using APL the Course Team would require students to prepare a report analysing the evaluating the prior industrial experience and this report would be assessed before the student enters Semester 6 and would be assessed in the same way as the assignment carried out by students completing the Industrial Placement Period. The Course Team would normally expect that a student will have been employed in horticulture for at least 48 weeks in order to qualify for APL. A satisfactory reference from the employer would also be required for consideration for APL.

10. Students must produce a placement report of a satisfactory standard to be allowed to continue with the course. However, the marks achieved will not contribute to the level of the award.

CANDIDATE'S CLAIM FORM FOR APCL

From November 1988 to September 1993, I was employed by a nursery company in Stratford-upon-Avon.

My responsibilities were the Production Control on two nurseries totalling 10.5 acres of Glass. I had to co-ordinate the production of the plug plants from sowing through to dispatch, with the help of one assistant. All in all my duties were:

• Recording estimated and actual germination
• Maintaining records and informing the customer of quantities available for sale.
• Monitoring and recording Integrated Pest Management
• Trailing and testing new plant varieties
• Organising the Duty Weekend Rota, and supervising a staff of nine people
• Assisting in the Soil Analysis Laboratory.

APCL

1. Discuss aspects of the business and the running of the business enterprise.
2. Prepare a critical account of the full range of operations in which the enterprise is involved having seen or been exposed to as wide a range as possible.
3. Take responsibility for a small part of the operation of the enterprise.
4. Prepare a report on a specialist aspect of an enterprise in which you have been involved. Look at the subject in an integrated or research way so that the results can be used to the advantage of the 'enterprise'.
5. Make decisions on a technical/management front, if only of a minor nature and if the opportunity affords it, to take on a supervisory role.
6. To work in a team towards an enterprise goal.

7. Carry out horticultural and technical skills associated with the specialist 'enterprise' in which you have been involved.

Parts 1–4 are discussed in more detail below.

1. Discuss aspects of the business and the running of the business enterprise

The nursery is a family business, started over 60 years ago.
   The objectives of the business are to satisfy the customer in the following areas:

* Quality
* Quantity
* Timeliness.

That is, to produce the number of plants in the correct quantity, at the time the customer requires them and of the correct quality.
   The function of the business is the production of ornamental young plants.
The structure of the organisation:

Two Partners

Administration Manager   Nursery Manager

Assistant Manager Supervisors for
a) Box filling
b) Seeding
c) Watering
d) Gapping up/Pricking out
e) Dispatch

2. Prepare a critical account of the full range of operations in which the enterprise is involved having seen or been exposed to as wide a range as possible.

Mutual operation with one customer on supplier basis.
   Main operation is the production of ornamental plug plants for one customer and poinsettia.
   Secondary operations are producing poinsettia cuttings for another customer and poinsettia pot plants for the supermarkets.
   Also, selling direct to a few wholesalers, a small number of pot plants and bedding plants that have been grown on to assess their commercial viability and to keep staff employed during a quiet time of the year.
   Although not considered normal business practice to have only one main customer – in fact, this is not recommended at all as it is considered too risky to have 'all your eggs in one basket', this policy has worked very well for these two organisations.
   The enterprise concentrates on growing the plug plants to a very high standard and the customer on supplying the seed and selling the finished plug plants. By concentrating on the enterprises sections that each does well, they have both benefited.
   In 1988, the enterprise had a glasshouse area of 17,008 sq.m. Four years later, it had nearly doubled in size to 31,704 sq.m and is still being enlarged but at a slower rate, see Figure 1.

The customer's business was founded in 1962, by one man, who saw his drive for ultimate quality and innovative marketing processes reflected in a rapidly expanding business, which is served with fully automated production facilities at the largest plug production unit in the UK.

3. Take responsibility for a small part of the operation of the enterprise

My responsibilities were the monitoring and recording of the production of seedlings and plug plants from sowing through to dispatch on two nurseries, totalling 10.5 acres of glass. I achieved this with the help of one part-time assistant.

The customer orders were recorded in files on a computer; the Spring Files 1992 were:

PRODUCTION

File	Plants	Tray Size	No of Varieties	File	Plants	Tray Size	No of Varieties
1	Begonia	MP	14	*1	Special	PL165	
2	Impatiens	MP	21	*2	Special	PL165	
3	Lobelia	MP	14	*3	Special	PL165	
4	Petunia	MP	5	*4	Special	P	
5	Other	MP	7	*5	Special	MP	
6	Begonia	PL165 1	2	*6	Special	352	
7	Impatiens	PL165	24	*7	Special	63/80	
8	Petunia	PL165	42	*8			
9	Cyclamen	PL165	6	*9	Jumbos		
10	Other	PL165	22	*10	Special	340	
11	Geranium	PL165	23	*11	Special	73	
12	Geranium	SP80	14	*12	Special	J7	
14	Pot Plants	SP63/80	13	*14	Special	Starplug	
15	Cyclamen	SP63	23	*15			
16	Cyclamen	J7	12	*16			
17	Geranium	J7	14	*17			
18	Jumbos		8	*18			
19	Geranium	352	22	*19			
20	Cyclamen	352	17	*20			
21	Perennial		80	*21			
22	Begonia	340	12	*22	Amateur	SP80	11
23	Geranium	340	22	*23	Amateur	16	5
24	Petunia	340	21	*24	Amateur	250	2
25	Other	340	16	*25	Amateur	100	16
26	Impatiens	340	20	*26	NST		27
27		SP 80	5	*27	Amateur	140	95
28	YP Geranium	84/124	27	*28	Amateur	J7	41
29	YP Cyclamen	84/PP	60	*29	Amateur	35	21
30	YP Cyclamen	124	13	*30	Amateur		8

I was responsible for the Production and Amateur Files; my assistant did the Specials.

Every week the office staff printed from the computer the week's Sowing and Plant Sheets.

The Sowing Sheets (Appendix 1) were printed with details of variety, customer's code, week to be sown, quantity, tray size, number of seeds in a cell and the total number of trays required and the week of dispatch were hand written on.

With the sowing sheets were the batch labels that were put on the benches at sowing and the correct number of sticky labels that were stuck on the trays as they were being sown. This was given to the Sowing Team and when the seed had been sown, the Sower filled in the amount of trays that had been sown on the sowing sheet and on the Batch label. At the end of the week, all Sowing Sheets were given back to the office staff who recorded all the shortages of seed trays not sown and ordered replacement seed.

The sheets were then passed to me and I filed them, after recording on the Wall Sowing Chart (Appendix 2) the week sown written on the week of delivery, each week was written in a different colour. This would verify that seed was being sown each week and, if not, a check would be made to see if it was a computer error or cancelled order. When the germination assessment had been done, it was crossed off on the chart, therefore ensuring that no germinations were missed and at this stage the correct amount of seed was sown and any shortages were in the pipeline.

The Plant Sheets (Appendix 3) were printed with details of variety, customer's code, week to be pricked out or gapped up, quantity required and the total number of trays required and the week of dispatch was hand written on.

From these sheets, I recorded on the Wall Plant Sheet (Appendix 4) the delivery week in the week it was to be gapped up or pricked out. After gapping up or pricking out the delivery week number was crossed off the sheet, so a check could be kept that all the work was kept up to date.

After the plants were gapped up or pricked out, the number of completed trays were counted and recorded by me on the plant sheets. If there were more trays than required the extra was recorded in black and if less recorded in red on the sheets. The percentage was written on the sheet in green; this figure was also recorded on the Manager's Master File, which was kept in his office (Appendix 5). From this figure it was possible to see if the required amount was available for the customer in the week that it was ordered.

The actual amount was forwarded to the customer, usually weekly via their salesman on plant sheets or the figures could be faxed or phoned through if the matter was urgent.

Apart from the Sowing and Plant Sheets that were produced by the computer, I devised and implemented all other sheets and charts, to enable me to provide all the information required by the Manager on a day to day basis.

During the summer, a new programme was installed on the computer and the format for the Autumn Files was changed and some extra information added. The files for the autumn were:

Production and Specials

File	Plants	Tray Size
1	Geranium Century	SP80
2	Other	SP80
3	Poly/Prim	SP80
4	Geranium Century	PL165
5	Geranium Multibloom	PL165
6	Other	PL165
7	Pansy Universal	PL165
8	Pansy Turbo	PL165
9	Poly/prim	PL165
10	Viola	PL165
11	Ranunculus	ST240
12	Polyanthus	ST240
13	Primrose	ST240
14	Pansy (Magnum)	340
15	Pansy (Turbo)	340
16	Pansy (Ultima)	340
17	Pansy (Universal)	340
18	Other	Jumbo
19	Pansy	Jumbo
20	Poly/prim	Jumbo
21	Poinsettia	J7

Sowing Sheets, the extra information required was the lot number of the seed. The number of trays to be sown and the delivery week were now printed on the sheet. Plant sheets also had the number of trays required and the delivery week printed on.

4. How I implemented the monitoring and recording

Estimate Germinations

Every Monday morning I would check the Wall Sowing Chart and transfer the information onto my clipboard charts of the seedlings which would be ready for an estimate germination.

Then I would walk round the nursery to find the seedlings. Before doing the estimate germination, I would place upright all the Batch Labels, the Colour Codes and the Week Delivery Numbers on every bench, checking that they were all correct – if not I would replace with the correct ones. Then, I would do an estimate germination by picking three trays at random of each variety and counting the number of seedlings in each tray, dividing by the size of the tray and thus having an estimate of the number of plants that would grow into a finished product. E.g. for the 165 trays, 3 trays could have $103 + 148 + 117 = 367$ seedlings, divide by 495 (165 x 3) = 0.74 x 100 = 74%. If a very large amount of trays of one variety were sown I would do more than one estimate germination and give a mean of the percentages. The percentage was recorded onto the clipboard sheet and later in the day transferred to the Master File. This was repeated for every variety, every week.

Whilst I was doing the estimate germination, I would note any problems such as large areas of empty trays or poor sowing or pest and disease problems and find out the cause and inform the Manager so that any shortfall in numbers was made up in later sowings.

Therefore, as there were 30 Production Files with a total number of 561 varieties and 9 Amateur Files with 226 varieties, this part of my responsibilities took up a great deal of my time, the busiest months being March and April.

Most of the plants were at the Stratford Nursery and the remainder were at the Welford Nursery; this involved a drive to Welford on Thursday morning to do the estimates and the counting there.

Actual Germinations

Every Monday after doing the Estimate Germination, I would do the Actual Germinations in a similar way.

Every afternoon, I walked round the nursery and counted the number of trays that had been gapped up that morning by the women. After I had counted each bench, I would place a marker in it so that it would not be counted twice. The number counted was recorded on a sheet and transferred, before the end of the afternoon, onto the Plant Sheet. When all figures had been recorded on the sheet it was passed on to the customer.

For the Master File, the gapped up and pricked out figures were changed into a percentage and recorded.

I worked out the percentage by dividing the gapped up or pricked out figure by the number sown and this gave the actual germination. E.g. Begonia Organdy Mix PL165, 93 trays gapped up divided by 105 trays sown x 100 = 88%.

Files 6-12 were gapped up, and Files 13–17 and 28–30 were pricked out. The counting of the pricked out plants was done by the person supervising the pricking out. This information was then passed on to me to do the actual germination for the Master File and to pass the figures available for sale to the customer.

Thus the estimate and the actual germinations could be seen together on one sheet in the Master File and compared with the germination that had been programmed into the computer. If they were all similar, production was as planned, but if there were any vast differences between the three, a problem had occurred and had to be rectified.

Appendix 1

Guidelines for Faculty Evaluators

TWO EXAMPLES

CLL values the acquisition of knowledge. In addition, learners should be challenged to develop high level thinking skills. Emphasis is placed, therefore, on analytical and integrative processes within our curriculum planning. Likewise in assessment, the learner has been guided to reflect on his or her experiences in terms of how learning takes place and why relationships are important.

It is useful to realise that there are different levels of thinking; how an individual operates depends upon training, experiences and developmental level. To assist you in focusing on evaluating prior learning, two of the categories from the cognitive taxonomy are defined in greater detail to highlight the characteristics learners may possess at different levels within each category.

Analytic thinking

High: Students high in analytic skills are quick to identify the essential components of ideas, events, problems and processes. They distinguish the important from the unimportant, fact from conjecture and make other distinctions imaginatively but usefully. They pick out deficiencies or inconsistencies in statements or positions. They are realistically sceptical or critical, but not destructively so.

Middle: Middle-level students find the essence of a problem or set of ideas through methodical effort rather than quick perception. They make useful distinctions among objects or ideas but not using unusual or imaginative methods. They find the obvious deficiencies in ideas or situations they are presented and effectively follow standard or accepted procedures to identify and solve problems. They are appropriately sceptical or critical but may miss a subtle inconsistency or fail to see unusual but available resolution of an apparent problem.

Low: Students low in analytical skills have difficulty getting beneath the surface of a problem, idea or a situation. They work with what they are presented, rarely dissecting it to examine the source or nature of the problem. They have difficulty distinguishing the essential from the unessential or making other discriminations that would simplify their task or lead to more effective solutions to a problem. They tend to be either uncritical, accepting what they are presented without question, or blindly critical, raising questions or objections that are neither well-found nor useful.

Example

The student is given two paragraphs from the report of the Personnel Security Board which considers charges that World War II physicist J. Robert Oppenheimer is a security risk. One paragraph summarises the majority view that government security and the national self interest takes precedence over individual rights of citizens. The student is to state the issue presented by the two opposing views.

Responses
High: The issue is stated clearly as the continuing struggle between personal freedom and national security.

Middle: The issue is not clearly stated. Either national security or personal freedom is discussed, but the two view points are not presented as separate. The response is mixed, having both justifiable and unquestioned selections of statements without reasons for their selection.

Low: The response only restates points made in one or both of the paragraphs without identification of the issue.

Integrative thinking or synthesising

High: Students with a high degree of synthesising skill are adept at organising apparently unrelated ideas into a common frame of reference. They find unifying themes or common threads that let them deal effectively with diffuse bodies of information. Facility at constructing a general framework to accommodate whatever information – applying its principles in new situations, generalising to other bodies of information or extrapolating from given to unknown situations. In short, they synthesise what they know into more general intellectual structures that they can bring to bear on new problems.

Middle: Students at an average of synthesising make connections between ideas when they are apparent or have been pointed out. Having seen the connections, they can then apply them and may also make similar connections among ideas or make useful generalisations much beyond the given material. They grasp most of the material presented them either in the classroom or textbook, but may have difficulty with highly complex or abstract concepts.

Low: The students low in skill have difficulty transferring ideas into higher order abstractions. They may grasp what is presented to them at the moment but do not readily integrate the current ideas with what has gone before or appreciate their ramifications in other situations. Their generalisations are often faulty, resulting from a quick focus on one or two salient points rather than one more complete understanding.

Example

Fifteen characteristics of federal government that refer to the branches of government and the elaboration of checks and balances are listed. The student is to describe both a strength and a weakness of the federal government as determined by the list.

Responses
High: The response describes the value of checks and balances and the problems of divided responsibility and authority that accompany them.

Middle: The answer makes a valid statement about the federal government, but does not relate it clearly to the given statements.

Low: A single statement in the list is discussed without a general statement being made.

QUESTIONING TECHNIQUES

As an evaluator, your job will be easier for you if you prepare some questions before the assessment meeting. There are a variety of ways to find out how much the learner knows, how he or she learns and applies this knowledge.

This last section integrates types of techniques with actual questions that have been asked during assessment meetings. From these examples, you can then go back to the Cognitive Taxonomy as you read through the learner's portfolio and identify the information you are interested in exploring. The meeting is an opportunity for the learner to elaborate upon, clarify or explain in more detail the content areas presented in the written document.

We make every attempt to structure the meeting as a non-threatening, educational experience. Assessment teams are supportive and seek to guide the learner in realising his or her strengths and limitations. Part of the function of the team is to recommend appropriate new learning experiences to assist the learner in acquiring a complete understanding of the academic and professional areas being pursued.

A portfolio may contain a range of credit requests which may be applied to several different areas. Because adult learners have been active in work, organisations and other activities, learning may be identified in academic areas of general education, electives or major areas of concentration/specialisation. Therefore, a team may consist of professionals and faculty from different fields as well. Your responsibility will be to look closely at the areas which match your own expertise for content and depth in understanding. Looking at other areas will afford you with the total picture of how the learner organises, analyses and evaluates information and experience.

The following techniques have been adapted from *Compendium of Assessment Techniques*, The Council for Adult and Experimental Learning (CAEL), 1974.

Simulation

A candidate is asked to pretend that he or she is engaged in some realistic task, the content described before the individual becomes involved. This technique offers the team the opportunity to assess responses in a life-like situation. Qualities such as decision-making, leadership, analytical thinking, planning skills and others may be observed.

Structure:

1. Instructions must be clear so that the candidates knows what is expected.
2. As designer of the exercise, you must have a thorough knowledge of the job or situation being simulated.
3. Tasks included in the excursus should not require knowledge that the candidate is not ordinarily expected to have.

Example

You are a first Line Manager in a small production company that manufactures plastic containers; you have been informed by upper management that your company will be implementing Management-By-Objectives. How would you go about explaining this to your workers and involving them in planning for the next quarter using this system?

Standard interview

In an interview, the candidate is asked questions designed to obtain answers related to one or more of the learning competencies being submitted for review. It is an interpersonal, open-ended technique which allows team members to explore content and factual knowledge as well as conceptual understandings. Questions can be phrased which directly correlate to the levels of *Bloom's Cognitive Taxonomy*.

Structure:

1. Questions should be directly related to knowledge submitted in the portfolio.
2. Questions should be appropriate, clear and unambiguous.
3. Learners should not be expected to reveal personal information.
4. Questions should not be leading or slanted so that the candidate offers a socially acceptable response.

Example

What are the stages involved in developing a new product? (Knowledge)
Explain your role in control. (Comprehension).
What are the weaknesses of your budget planning process? (Analysis)
How did you assess need, develop and set up your human services clinic? (Synthesis)
Why was this final decision made and why this over other possibilities? (Evaluation)

Case study

This is a fairly complete and realistic statement of some problem which can be related to business, human services or any other area. The candidate is asked to present an analysis of the problem. It is a useful technique in assessing an individual's ability to analyse and solve problems.

Structure:

1. The case study should be prepared and presented to the learner prior to the team meeting.
2. The situation must be appropriate to the knowledge presented by the learner.
3. Because all assessment team members are entitled to adequate time for questioning, the learner's response to the case study should be limited and sufficient. Therefore, you should design the case study with this in mind.

Example

A Director of a Day Care Centre in Concord, New Hampshire has been notified of a reduction in state welfare money for children of dependent families. Approximately 25 per cent of the operating budget has come from Title XX monies. Enrolment from tuition paying clients has decreased 5 per cent over the past six months. There are four other centres in Concord offering care for children of three years to school age. The Board of this centre has considered expanding services to include after school care. There will be no funds available from the state to implement any changes. Faced with the present situation, what action should the Director take and why?

Role playing

Situations set up for role playing involve a person-to-person confrontation characteristic of work in any field. The candidate would assume a role as described by you, with you also playing a part. Other team members might be drawn into participating as well. Role playing identifies specific behaviour in addition to content and knowledge.

Structure:

1. The instructions and roles must be clearly defined by you as the team member initiating the exercise.
2. The content of the situation should be appropriate to the type of prior experience the learner has had in the field.
3. Role playing must be timed so as not to monopolise an unnecessary proportion of the assessment meeting.

Example

Let's say I'm a retailer in computers. You are a Sales Representative for a company that deals in mini computers and full size systems. My operation is interested in expanding our market. This is our first meeting. How would you approach me?

Product assessment

This technique evaluates samples the candidate may present at the time of the meeting. Reference may be made to these products in the portfolio such as drawings, paintings, graphics or photographs. Since the products represent a skill the candidate possesses, this technique is an indirect procedure.

Structure:

1. The product(s) may be available for the first time at the team meeting and if so, adequate time must be allowed for viewing and evaluation.
2. Questions that are posed to the candidates would be qualitative in nature and be directed at the process, techniques and rationale used to create the product(s).
3. Because judgements may be subjective in viewing creative work, standards or criteria should be established prior to examining the samples. These should be available to the learner as part of the evaluation process.

Example

A candidate is requesting credit for her knowledge of painting. She has included a description of her experiences, technical knowledge and photographs of her work. At the meeting she presents an oil, water-colour and pen and ink drawing. Questions asked might include: What do you see as the similarities and differences between oils and water-colours? Tell me about the selection of subject matter and composition of your picture. Describe the techniques that you used. What would you do differently if you were to attempt these pieces again?

APL Statistical and Monitoring Log

Applicant	Date of applying	CAMS	Module codes	No. of credits.	Date APL assessed	Credits agreed	Nature of evidence	Stage or year entered

Appendix 3

Function of the APL Regulatory Framework

Ideally any APL regulatory framework should ensure that:

- justice and fairness is carried out with respect to all applicants
- there is consistency of practice across the institution both in terms of the advice given to applicants and in the identification of the number and level of credits awarded
- the control of subject-specific accreditation resides with the subject areas concerned
- the APL system is managed, monitored and evaluated centrally, and is subject to external verification
- normal admission issues are separated from APL
- normal CATS or CAMS issues (where standing agreements for transfer exist between programmes and/or institutions) should be articulated within the framework
- applications are dealt with as efficiently as possible having particular regard to clear communications and feedback to applicants.

Submission of a Claim (Illustrative Example)

SUBMISSION OF CLAIM

All prospective students will submit their APL applications through a designated point (e.g. centrally through Admissions Officer or registry). Like assignments, applications may normally be submitted at a particular point before the start of the programme or module for which credit is being sought. If submission deadlines differ from programme to programme or from academic level to academic level this must be made explicit well in advance.

Arrangements should be in place for dealing with exceptional circumstances such as genuine extenuating circumstances. This is important as these applicants will and should have the right of appeal under the institutional appeals procedures.

Submitted portfolios should be distributed to the appropriate programme teams as soon as practicable and within an agreed time scale.

Assessors (often the subject specialists) will determine the specific academic credit that would, in their view, be appropriate to the claim. The assessors will normally invite the applicant to attend for an APL interview.

The decision of the assessors must be communicated to the applicant in writing as soon as possible.

The decision of the APL assessors should be reviewed by significant others including external examiners as agreed by the institution. The final agreed outcome must be recorded centrally for purposes of statistics and quality assurance.

Appendix 5

Summary of Organisational Factors

STAGE OF APEL	ORGANISATIONAL FACTORS
PRE-OPERATIONAL STAGE	
Initial Development of APEL system The aim is to ensure valid and credible APEL system	– organisational agreement/policy of APEL – identification of development funds liaison with academic registry and accreditation body – appointment of APEL development officer – early establishment of APEL committee and APEL mechanism – development of training for staff
OPERATIONAL STAGE	
The aim is to provide guidance for prospective candidates	– development of publicity information – development of collective use of APEL mechanism – standardisation of procedure for APEL – identification of marketing budget – consultation with CATS committee and accrediting institution – establishment of an assessment criteria – establishment of good practice in APEL – negotiation with workplace and give credit where credit is due
EVALUATION STAGE	
The aim is to offer a critical review of pre-operational and operational stages of APEL	– evaluate the APEL techniques and mechanism being used and offer ways of improving them – evaluate the adequacy and usefulness of the pre-operational stage – assess future needs and plan accordingly – assess candidates' need to acquire portfolio presenting skills and how this may be credited

Illustrative Flow Chart

ORGANISATIONAL FACTORS: APL OPEN EVENT

Corporate agreement to hold open event

*   venue (off campus in community and/or on campus), booking made and confirmed
*   date and time

Notification and agreement for staff to attend

*   academic (including senior staff representation if appropriate)
*   clerical/registry services
*   portering staff
*   marketing department representation

Promotional material devised, produced and distributed

*   agree mode of promotional material e.g. leaflet/newspaper/advertisement
*   agree target group
*   agree and compile 'copy' i.e. text for promotional material
*   generate design style
*   agree response device e.g. freepost reply/free phone number
*   final check of design and contents of promotional material
*   print and distribute (leaflets) and/or place advertisements

Monitor response from promotional material and estimate numbers likely to attend

Book and confirm catering facilities

Generate display of directional material and estimate numbers likely to attend

Confirm arrangements with staff attending

Arrange for transportation and set-up of display and publicity materials to venue

Evaluate/obtain feedback on open event and use future planning

*   monitor numbers attending
*   level of follow-up/ongoing
*   number of firm applications

Produced by and reproduced with permission of S Low, Marketing Manager,
Worcester College of Higher Education.

Appendix 6

Abbreviations

ACE	American Council on Education
APCL	Assessment of Prior Certificated Learning
APEL	Assessment of Prior Experiential Learning
APL	Assessment of Prior Learning
BTEC	Business & Technology Education Council
CAEL	Council for Adult and Experiential Learning
CAMS	Credit Accumulation & Modular Scheme
CATS	Credit Accumulation & Transfer Scheme
CLEP	College Level Examination Programme
C & G	City & Guild
CNAA	Council for National Academic Awards (until 31 March 1992)
CVCP	Committee of Vice-Chancellors & Principals
DES	Department of Education & Science (until 1992)
DQA	Division of Quality Audit
ENB	English National Board
GNVQ	General National Vocational Qualification
HEFCE	Higher Education Funding Council for England
HEQC	Higher Education Quality Council
IPD	Institute of Personnel Development
MCI	Management Charter Initiative
MidCAT	Midland Consortium for Credit Accumulation and Transfer
MTL	Multimedia Teaching & Learning
MYEC	Making Your Experience Count
NCET	National Council for Educational Technology
NIACE	National Institute of Adult Continuing Education
NVQ	National Vocational Qualification
OU	Open University
PLA	Prior Learning Assessment
RSA	Royal Society of Arts
TDLB	Training Directorate Lead Body
TQI	Total Quality Improvement
TQM	Total Quality Management
UDACE	Unit for the Development of Adult Continuing Education (until 1992)
WBL	Work Based Learning

Example of a Portfolio for the TDLB Standards

INTRODUCTION

A lead industry body is drawn from practitioners of a specific skill – in the case outlined this is for teaching and learning across a range of sectors. The lead industry body's remit is to set up standards for best practice, therefore the achievement of relevant national vocational qualifications (NVQ) is fundamental to anyone practising as a trainer.

The training directorate lead body qualification is required for teaching, designing learning strategies and particularly in the assessment of students and strategies for learning.

TDLB have therefore designed standards which are used by a variety of award bodies as part of their portfolio, notably:

- Institute Personal Development (IPD)
- City and Guilds (C & G)
- Business and Technical Education Council (BTEC)
- Royal Society of Arts (RSA) etc.

The awarding bodies then license centres which conform to their quality assurance criteria. It is then the centres' responsibility to ensure for whatever vocational qualifications they are offering that those administering the qualification are themselves vocationally competent as described by the TDLB standards within their own vocational practice area. While there is obviously commonality of approach in designing and assessing NVQs, it should be recognised that fundamental vocational skills are however not in themselves transferable. For example, a qualified plumber would not be expected to assess competence in catering.

THE STANDARDS

The TDLB defined the Key Purpose of training and development as:

> develop human potential to assist organisations and individuals to achieve their objectives

This statement reflects training and development's dual role to assist both organisations and individuals. But what does all this mean and how can it be done in practice? To answer this question the Lead Body adopted the Systematic Training Cycle to define areas of competence.

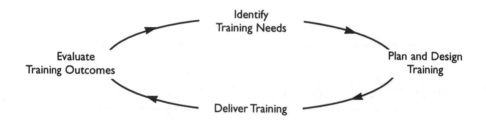

Figure 12 *The systematic training cycle*

The cycle was chosen because:

* it describes systematically and comprehensively the whole training and development process.
* it is familiar in all sectors and to all parts of the training community.
* most training and development roles can be located within it.

The Systematic Training Cycle still forms the basis of the revised functional map, which attempts to describe the functions carried out by trainers.

The Key Purpose is split into five AREAS OF COMPETENCE which, when taken together, constitute the achievement of the Key Purpose. You will see that Areas A, B, C and E correspond to distinct stages of the Systematic Training Cycle. Area D corresponds to the assessment and progress of individuals only. It comprises the assessment and verification units, which are the cornerstones of the NVQ Quality Assurance System.

PORTFOLIO EXAMPLE

This qualification is traditionally gained by preparation of a portfolio of evidence in one of two manners. Firstly, by the new practitioner who will undertake a structured development programme and in the course of this gradually build examples of performance in compliance to the relevant TDLB standards. Secondly, by established practitioners who may apply for accreditation of prior experimental learning (APEL), again assessing a portfolio of evidence drawn from practice undertaken during the past three years.

The following example shows how the same evidence given in Chapter 7 has been used in this case by the tutor/advisor to gain the TDLB standards.

The five areas of competence are split into 14 sub-areas, as shown in the diagram on page 6. Each sub-area is further broken down into a number of UNITS OF COMPETENCE, which are, in turn, composed of two or more ELEMENTS OF COMPETENCE, which include associated performance criteria (the national standards). For example:

The tutor in this scenario has previously submitted work to be assessed against the TDLB standards (D32, 33 and 36). Additional evidence was requested to confirm competence in dealing with one candidate through a D33 process (assessing candidate using diverse sources of evidence).

Previous portfolio entries of the tutor contained the new standard format of cross referencing matrices, personal report/narrative/story-based and the evidence itself. This uses the same methodology as that given in Chapter 7.

The additional evidence as requested by the summative assessor was in this case listed and appended to the portfolio without the additional story board/narrative.

TDLB D33 Additional Evidence Requested

In addition to Cameo 4 (D34 Candidate assessment) formative assessment of an NVQ4 management portfolio is offered authorised by Patricia Davis of Nottingham City Council.

Evidence No.

Patricia is enrolled on the BTEC NVQ4 programme	I
Portfolio for units 2,3,4,5,8 and 9 received 9/2/95	2
Desktop assessment carried out (CC7)	3
Questions posed for candidate's attention (18/2)(CC8)	4
Candidate's written and oral responses recorded (19/5)	5
Summary of assessment made (CC/msmorsQ94)	6
Previous IV acknowledgement of unit certification	7 a&b

This extends coverage of additional elements assessed and covers the essences of:

> D331 Planning
> D332 Questioning/evaluation
> D333 Decision-making/feedback

PORTFOLIO AVAILABLE FOR INSPECTION AS REQUIRED

ASSESSOR REPORT: (Continued)

Unit 3.1 Evidence 73 (Report)
Well-presented information and appropriate evidence.

Evidence 01
Provides evidence of targets but without obvious financial details. However the links to financial implications can be seen. This really is secondary but still very relevant evidence.

Evidence 77
Good evidence but its link to Patricia unclear.

Evidence 86
Good evidence with clear links to formal planning.

K&U   Comments relevant showing a clear appreciation of data gathering and problem solving with context of financial resource discussions. Financial analysis tools need further exploration.

Range (3.1)
The links to range need clarifying in particular that of 'working conditions'.

Unit 3.2

Evidence 79 (Report)
Unclear how evidence 08 meets performance criteria claimed. The relevance and potential can be appreciated but the specific reference to the pc's needs putting.

Evidence 80
Shows a requisition form, pc 'c' is not obvious. Patricia's direct involvement on this piece of evidence is unclear.

Evidence 81 a&b
The example looks relevant but does not quite match the narrative. The extensive pc's claimed require more justifications.

Evidence 82/83
Appropriate to claims but it would have been appropriate to show an example

Evidence 84
pc 'f' unclear.

Evidence 85
Relevant.

Assessor Signature .... Date ....

Page .3.. of .9..

FORM CC7A   CANDIDATE REGISTRATION NO. ....

Formative

ASSESSMENT OF PORTFOLIO

Candidate .... Level ....

ASSESSOR REPORT: (Continued)

Evidence 86 (including 84,87,88,89,90).
Relevant argument concerning budgetary processes showing extensive pre-coverage.

Evidence 91 (including 92,93,94).
Good example of control measures backed up with evidence.

K&U   Well-stated people involvement in the financial control arena.

Range (3.2)
Range coverage would appear complete but needs indicating. Perhaps the policy statement of the organisation expectations of their management and limits of authority would be relevant.

Generally evidence sets 86 and 91 are good. Some clarification of 79 report and associated evidence is required to confirm relevance to pc's claimed.

The outcome of Y9's explanations with possibly some supporting documentation should suffice for Unit 3.2.

Assessor Signature .... Date ....

Page .4.. of .9..

FORM CC7A   CANDIDATE REGISTRATION NO. ....

Formative

ASSESSMENT OF PORTFOLIO

Candidate .... Level ....

ASSESSOR REPORT: (Continued)

Unit 4.1

Evidence 41
Report

Evidence 42 (Witness Testimony)

The report 2/11 does not really address pc 'a' or lead you to 'd' as such.

Evidence 44
There are only loose links to pc 'a' here.

Evidence 45
Good coverage but a specific 'personal specification' not immediately apparent.

K&U   Again an excellent report showing a distinct people commitment. Good to see move
       towards competencies. Statement of linking personal skills to job skills made but no real
       evidence presented to support this claim, this being a K&U requirement rather than pc-
       based.

Range
The relevance to range needs highlighting to ensure full coverage is present. Perhaps indication as to
the organisation's adherence/commitment to equal opportunities might be highlighted (in Section 1?).

Unit 4.2
All evidence. An extremely thorough analysis supported with evidence covering all pc areas.

K&U   Indicate a depth of understanding of the subject and a deep commitment in providing an
       extremely high-quality, caring selection process.

Range
Indication of full range coverage is required but no gaps would appear to be present.
With exception of range 4.1 comment a very thorough coverage 4.1/4.2.

Assessor Signature   .... Date   ....

Page .5.. of .9..

FORM CC7A   CANDIDATE REGISTRATION NO.   ....

Formative

ASSESSMENT OF PORTFOLIO

Candidate   .... Level   ....

ASSESSOR REPORT: (Continued)

Unit 5.1

Evidence 1&9 Report 122/124
Evidence included is difficult to link to pc's a&b and c apart from on one occasion.

Evidence 128
Report shows an excellent method of team building and highlights pc's a&b really well.

Range
It is unclear what involvement there has been with higher level managers and needs addressing suit-
ably.
A high level of training has been evidenced but its necessity and timing are not clear.

Unit 5.2

Evidence 131 (Report)

Assessor Signature   .... Date   ....

FORM CC7A   CANDIDATE REGISTRATION NO.   ....

Formative ASSESSMENT OF PORTFOLIO

Candidate   .... Level   ....

Element:		Question:	Response:
3	QI	Justification of points on CC7A pg are required for evidence set 79.	See reply in file OK with evidence in 66;67;73;74a TCR 7-6-95
	Q2	Prepare a *brief* resume either written or for verbal presentation showing how PERSONAL SPECS as well as JOB SPECS need to be accounted for in recount and selectors	See reply in file Range indicated of unit introduction and of each evidence.
	Q3		Witness testimony or observation by Advisor.
	Q4		Line manager to sign, see justification in file OK TCR 7/6
	Q5		See K&U in report 73 accepted TCR 7/6

DATE ASSESSMENT INTERVIEW PLAN (CC8) SENT TO CANDIDATE:

Assessor Signature   .... Date   ....

FORM CC7A   CANDIDATE REGISTRATION NO.   ....

Formative ASSESSMENT OF PORTFOLIO

Candidate   .... Level   ....

Element:		Question:	Response:
3	QI	Justification of points on CC7A pg are required for evidence set 79.	See justification sheets 08,80,81a+b, 84 accepted TCR 7/7
	Q2	Prepare a *brief* resume either written or for verbal presentation showing how PERSONAL SPECS as well as JOB SPECS need to be accounted for in recount and selectors.	Covered in 4.2 evidence TCR
	Q3	In earlier documented training sessions how did you define the relevance as read for the training. How was higher management involved.	See K & U 51-53
	Q4	Could you provide evidence as to how training roles needs and reviews (suitably agreed on) link to operational/individual requirements.	See response in file OK but an interview may be accepted TCR
	Q5		

DATE ASSESSMENT INTERVIEW PLAN (CC8) SENT TO CANDIDATE:

Assessor Signature   .... Date   ....

Bibliography

Allen, M. (1988) *The Goals of Universities*. The Society for Research into Higher Education and Open University Press, Milton Keynes

Ball, C. (1989) *Aim Higher Widening Access to Higher Education*. Interim Report Matters, RSA

Barnett, R. (1990) *The Idea of Higher Education*. The Society for Research into Higher Education and The Open University Press, Milton Keynes

Beattie, A. (1987) Making a Curriculum Work, in Allen, P. and Jolley, M. (eds) *The Curriculum in Nursing Education*. London: Croom Helm

Beaumont, G. (1995) *Review of 100 NVQs and SVQs*. Report for the Department for Education and Employment, Evaluation and Advisory Group (EAG)

Becher (1989) *Academic Tribes and Territories*. The Society for Research into Higher Education and The Open University Press, Milton Keynes

Biggs, J. B. (1991) Teaching: Design for Learning Higher Education Research and Development, in Atkins, M. J., Beattie, J. and Dockrell, W. B. (1993) *Assessment Issues in Higher Education*. School of Education Newcastle Upon Tyne and Employment Department, Further and Higher Education

Bullough, R. (1989) A Consideration of Some Models of the Learning Process: Variations on a theme of John Dewey. *Studies in the Education of Adults*, 21(2), 81–116

Butterworth, C. (1992) More Than One Bite at APEL: Contrasting Models of Accrediting Prior Learning. *Journal of Further and Higher Education*, 16(3)

Challis, M. (1993) *Introducing APL*. London: Routledge

City & Guilds (1990) *APL handbook: guidance on the accreditation of prior learning*. London: City & Guilds

Cohen, R. and Whitaker, U. (1994) Chapter Two: Assessing Learning from Experience Perspectives on Experiential Learning, Prelude to a Global Conversation about Learning. *International Experiential Learning Conference Papers*. CAEL's 20 Anniversary International Conference, November 1994: Washington DC, USA

Davis, B. D. and Burnard, P (1992) Academic Levels in Nursing. *Journal of Advanced Nursing*, 17, 1395–1400

Dearing, R. (1996) *Review of qualifications for 16–19 year olds*. Middlesex: SCAA Publications

Deming, W. E. (1986) *Out of the Crisis*. Boston: Massachusetts

Department for Education (1993) *Higher Quality and Choice, the Charter of Higher Education: Raising the Standard*. London: DfE

Dixon, S. (1993) Immeasurable Waste of Human Talent. *Financial Times*, 7th July, p 11

Dreyfus, S. and Dreyfus, H. (1980) *A Five Stage Model of the Mental Activities Involved in Direct Skill Acquisition*. University of California, Berkeley

English, L. (1992) Children's Domain Specific Knowledge and Domain General

Strategies in Problem Solving. *British Journal of Educational Psychology* 62, 203–216

English National Board (ENB) (1997) *An investigation into the reliability and validity of assessment strategies for the accreditation of prior learning of nurses, midwives and health visitors.* A final report written by the South East England Consortium (SEEC) for credit accumulation and transfer

Evans, N. (1988) *Handbook for the Assessment of Experiential Learning.* Learning From Experience Trust

Evans, N. (1992) *Experiential Learning: Assessment and Accreditation.* London: Routledge

Faltermeyer, T. (1994) The Higher Award – Assessing at Different Levels. *Senior Nurse,* 13(7), 32–36

Fenwick, A., Assister, A. and Nixon, N. (1992) *Profiling in Higher Education: Guidelines for the Development of Profiling Schemes.* Employment Department and Council for National Academic Awards

Field, M. (1993) *APL, Developing More Flexible Colleges.* London: Routledge

Firkwood, R. (1994) Importance of Assessment Learning, cited in Murray, P. (1996) Portfolios and Accreditation of Prior Experimental Learning (APEL) Make Credits or Problems? *Nurse Education Today,* 14(3), 232–237

Fox, J., Nyatanga, L., Ringer, C and Greaves, J. (1992) APL, A Corporate Strategy. *Nurse Education Today,* 12(3), 221–226

Frain, J. (1981) *Introduction to Marketing.* Plymouth: MacDonald & Evans

Fugate, M. and Chapman, R. (1992) *Prior Learning Assessment: Result of a Nationwide Institutional Survey.* Chicago: CAEL

Fulton, D. and Ellwood, S. (1989) *Admission to Higher Education: Policy and Practice.* Lancaster Training Agency

Further and Higher Education Act (1992). London: HMSO

Gipps, C. and Stobart (1993) *Assessment: A Teachers Guide.* London: Hodder and Stoughton

Glen, S. and Hight, N. (1992) Portfolios: An Effective Assessment Strategy. *Nurse Education Today,* 12(6), 416–423

Greatorex, J. and Nyatanga, L. (1994) *Academic Levels in the Accreditation of Prior Learning.* CAEL: International Conference, Washington DC, USA (unpublished)

Hall, D. (1993) Conference Paper: *Awarding Students Credit for Prior Experiential Learning Whilst Protecting Academic Standards.* Conference: A Practical Guide to APEL, held at University of Greenwich, 31 March 1993

HEQC (1994) *Checklist for Quality Assurance Systems.* London: HEQC

HEQC (1997) *Graduate Standards Programme: Assessment in Higher Education and the Role of Graduates.* London: HEQC

Hillier, J. (Chief Executive) (1966) *The Monitor,* Autumn, National Council for Vocational Qualifications

Kaplan, A. (1988) *Postmodernism and its Discontents: Theories, Practices.* London: Verso

Kerrigan, K. (1991) Decision Making in Today's Complex Environment. *Nursing Administration Quarterly,* 15(4), 1–5

Knapp, J. and Gardner, M. (1981) Assessment Of Prior Learning: As a Model and in Practice, in Keeton, M. T. (ed.) *New Directions in Experiential Learning.* San Francisco: Jossey-Bass

Koch, T. (1992) A Review of Nursing Quality Assurance. *Journal of Advanced Nursing,* 17, 785–794

Lamdin, L. (1991) *Roads to the Learning Society*. Council for Adult and Experiential Learning

Lamdin, L. (1992) *Earn College Credits for What You Know* (2nd edn). Chicago: CAEL

Mandl, C. T. *et al.* (1991) *Learning and Instruction: European Research in an International Context*. USA: Peragon Press

MCI (1991) *Management standards: Implementation pack*. London: Management Charter Initiative

McKelvey, C. H. and Peters, H. (1993) *APL: Equal Opportunities for All?* London: Routledge

Mitchell, M. (1994) The Views of Students and Teachers on the Use of Portfolios as a Learning and Assessing Tool in Midwifery Education. *Nurse Education Today*, 14, 38–43

NCVQ (1992) *National Standards for Assessment and Verification*. London

Nyatanga, L. (1991) CATS, APEL and ET: The Vital Link. *Senior Nurse*, (1), 26–29

Nyatanga, L. (1993) APL: Some International Perspectives. *The British Journal of Nursing*, 2(18), 892-893

Nyatanga, L. and Forman, D. (1997) Accreditation of prior learning (APL) and multidisciplinary issues. *CAEL Forum*, 21(1), 8–10, 34

Nyatanga, L. and Fox, J. (1992) *Good Practice in the Accreditation of Prior Learning: Report of the Research Project*: November 1990–June 1992. University of Derby/MIDCAT

Nyatanga, L. and Fox, J. (1993) Placing APL on the agenda. *Senior Nurse*, 13(2), 23–24

Nyatanga, L. and Fox, J. (1996) Assessment of Prior Learning: The Drives. *Council for Adult & Experiential Learning (CAEL) Forum*, 19(4), 15–16, 32

Open University (1990) *The Accreditation of Prior Learning: A Training Pack for Advisors and Assessors*. School of education, Centre for Youth and Adult Studies. Open University Course P528

Otter, S. (1991) *What Can Graduates Do? A Consultative Document*. UDACE, NIACE

Paulson, L. F. and Paulson, P. R. (1989) *How Do Portfolios Measure Up? A Cognitive Model For The Assessment Of Portfolios*. North West Evaluation Association

Quinn, F. M. (1994) The Demise of the Curriculum, Chapter Two, in Humphreys, J. and Quinn, F. M. (1994) *Health Care Education: The Challenge of the Market*. London: Chapman and Hall

Ramsden, P. (1979) Student Learning and Perceptions of the Academic Environment. *Higher Education*, 8(4), 411–427

Redfern, E. and James, C. (1994) Conference Paper: *Credits, Levels and Professional Learning – Some Considerations*. Nurse Education Tomorrow 5th Annual International Participative Conference, St. Mary's College University of Durham, September 6–8 1994

Robbins, Lord (1963) *Higher Education CMND 2154*. London: HMSO

Robertson, D. (1994) *Choosing to change: extending access, choice and mobility in higher education*. Report of the Higher Education Quality Council (HEQC) Credit Accumulation and Transfer (CAT) Development Project

Rogers, E. M. and Shoemacher, F. F. (1971) *Communication of Innovation* (2nd edn). New-York: Free Press

Ryle, G. (1949) *The Concept of Mind*. London: Hutchinson

Schuller, T. (1995) (ed.) *The Changing University*. The Society for Research into Higher Education & OU Press, Milton Keynes

Simosko, S. (1988) *Assessing Learning: a CAEL handbook for faculty*. Council for Adult and

Experiential Learning, Maryland

Simosko, S. (1991) *APL: A Practical Guide for Professionals*. Kogan Page: London

Smithers, A. and Robinson, P. (1989) *Increasing Participation in Higher Education*. School of Education, University of Manchester, BP Educational Services

Tappen, R. M. (1995) *Nursing Leadership and Management Concepts and Practice*. Philadelphia, USA: F A Davies

Toyne, P. (1979) *Educational Credit Transfer: feasibility study*. DES

Usher, R. and Edwards, R. (1994) *Postmodernism and Education*. London: Routledge

Whitaker, U. (1989) *Assessing Learning: Standards, Principles and Procedures*. Chicago: CAEL

Winter, R. (1993) The Problem of Educational Levels (Part 1): Conceptualising a Framework for Credit Accumulation and Transfer. *Journal of Further and Higher Education*, 17(3), Autumn

Wolf, A. (1995) *Competency Based Assessment*. Buckingham: Open University Press

Index